Improving
Urban Middle Schools

IMPROVING URBAN MIDDLE SCHOOLS

Lessons from the Nativity Schools

L. MICKEY FENZEL

STATE UNIVERSITY OF NEW YORK PRESS

Published by
STATE UNIVERSITY OF NEW YORK PRESS, ALBANY

© 2009 State University of New York

For information, contact State University of New York Press, Albany, NY
www.sunypress.edu

Production by Laurie Searl
Marketing by Michael Campochiaro

Library of Congress Cataloging-in-Publication Data

Fenzel, L. Mickey, 1949-
    Improving urban middle schools : lessons from the Nativity schools / L. Mickey Fenzel.
       p. cm.
    Includes bibliographical references and index.
    ISBN 978-0-7914-9349-6 (hardcover : alk. paper)
    ISBN 978-0-7914-9350-2 (pbk. : alk. paper)
1. Education, Urban—United States—Case studies. 2. Educational change—United States—
Case studies. 3. Church and education—United States—Case studies. 4. NativityMiguel
Network of Schools. I. Title.
    LC5131.F46 2009
    370.9173'2—dc22

                                                                    2008025082

                        10   9   8   7   6   5   4   3   2   1

To my first teachers:
my father, Leo F. Fenzel, Sr.,
and my mother, Adrienne Malloy (Eberly) Fenzel

Contents

List of Tables

Foreword

America is, without question, a nation of urban schools. Some 11 million children, about one-quarter of all students in public education, attend an urban school—a number which includes 43 percent of the nation's minority school-goers and 35 percent of its poor. The centrality of racial-cultural diversity and economic disadvantage in the discourse about the performance of urban schools has led many to read the term "urban education" as "poor and minority city schooling." In the recent years there have been a plethora of books, articles and monographs purporting to address the trenchant persistent issues related to underperforming urban schools. Both professional and popular literatures reveal a growing preoccupation with the association of these social contextual factors with the depressed performance of urban schools.

Few Americans are unfamiliar with the phrase "achievement gap" or how it dominates the discourse on addressing the needs of poor and minority students. According to a recent comprehensive study reported in the New York Times (July 5, 2005), poor students in urban schools in economically disadvantaged communities performed worst of any group with some two-thirds of them failing to reach the basic proficiency levels on national tests. In addition to this, minority children and youth, who constitute the majority of students in virtually every urban school system, are disproportionately placed in special education classes, formally disciplined with suspensions and expulsions, and adjudicated as criminals in zero-tolerance school policies. For all the volumes of scholarly articles, papers, books and reports on improving urban teaching and learning, we as a nation do not seem to have made very much headway. If there is a useful thread for improving the educational experience of children and youth attending urban schools, it is the growing realization that poverty and racial or cultural status do not *cause* academic underperformance of individuals, but rather constitute conditions that more severely challenge the capacity of our educational systems to be as successful with poor and minority children as with their more economically advantaged, European American and culturally mainstream counterparts. That thread is a growing recognition that the quality of the social, academic and cultural environment of the day-to-day experience is a *necessary*, but not a *sufficient* condition to guarantee school attainment of the those traditionally least well served.

We know that a supportive, affirming and child-centered social environment is vital to the successful academic achievement and personal development of young people, so what we need now is a working knowledge of how conditions of their lives inside and outside school impact their academic performance. The relationship between these social and cultural conditions of urban school goers on the one hand and their school achievement performance on the other hand, would be far more productive with a deeper understanding *quality of the learning community* in urban school settings. The call for this deeper understanding of school community was articulated over four decades ago as a matter recovering the "missing community" (Newman & Oliver, 1967). The idea resurfaced more recently as a question of diminishing capacity to build and sustain community in American culture in general (Putnam, 2001).

This book breaks new ground in the attempt to articulate the needed reconstruction of the "missing community" and examines community as a process for addressing trenchant issues and problems of schooling, learning and development in urban schools. This book explains how the plight of urban education is informed by Nativity school model of middle school education. It reports the results of a multi-site, multi-city study of Nativity schools, and how the concept has evolved in its implementation over the 30 after the founding of the first Nativity school. This book documents the relationship between the unique features of Nativity schooling and enhanced levels of academic success and educational attainment. In a carefully crafted study, the Nativity schooling experience is contrasted with comparable urban middle schools to examine what school community factors matter, and how they have contributed to the success of the students. The results of the study indicate that Nativity schools provide middle schoolers in under-resourced urban communities with the tools and experiences they need to achieve at high levels.

This volume also advances the inquiry of the missing elements of the moral and ethical dimensions of community in the conversations about how to improve urban teaching and learning. Readers will see how the Nativity school experience pushes the envelope of our understanding of the critical social-contextual qualities in the learning environment and how they promote achievement and development. The work also poses some interesting issues that really need to be taken up by those interested in inquiry regarding the moral and ethical components of excellence in urban education. This volume identifies, explains and illustrates elements that account for higher academic performance and well being among students attending Nativity Schools in comparison to public and private match-mates. Anyone interested in learning how to create the conditions for a enabling sociocultural environment in under-resourced urban schools must read this book.

June 22, 2008
Peter C. Murrell, Jr., Ph.D.
Professor and Founding Dean, School of Education
Loyola College in Maryland

Acknowledgments

This initial foray into writing a book reflects the labor and love of many people who have guided and supported me. To these friends, family members, colleagues, and Nativity educators and students I owe many thanks for their support, encouragement, and insights.

First and foremost, Fr. Jack Podsiadlo, S. J., whom I consider to be Father Nativity, coauthored the second chapter of this book on the history of the Nativity schools. As the then director of the national Nativity Education Centers Network headquartered in Baltimore, he and Ms. Carol Hillery, his assistant, paved the way for me to visit the Nativity schools included in this study and provided me with data and other material about the schools and the Network. Fr. Jack was indeed an inspiration for this work. How fortunate I was that his office was located just a short drive from mine at Loyola College.

The presidents, principals, teachers, students, and other school personnel at the Nativity schools and local parochial schools who so graciously opened their school and classroom doors to me were my teachers in this project. I am grateful for the many friends I have made in the schools and the lessons I have learned from them in this endeavor.

My research partners and assistants at Loyola College in Maryland have contributed much to the collection and recording of data and the preparation of reports submitted to the Nativity Network and the participating schools in the study. First, I thank director Dr. Mark Peyrot and graduate assistant Kate Devlin, of the Center for Social and Community Research, who oversaw the entering of data from the hundreds of surveys completed by students and teachers. Graduate research assistants Janine Domingues, Stephen Toglia, Ros Monteith, and Gerivonni Flippen, and also Nora Riordan, contributed to data collection and analysis, and Benita St. Amant and June August transcribed interview recordings. I appreciate, too, colleagues and friends Kathy Sears and Dr. Janet Preis and my educator-daughter, Elizabeth Fenzel, who read drafts of sections of the book and offered valuable feedback. Also to be thanked are my colleagues in the Middle-Level Education Research SIG of the American Educational Research Association who have provided feedback on the papers I have presented at AERA conferences. Finally, I thank my mentors from my doctoral program years at Cornell University, Dr. Steve Hamilton and Dr. George Posner, under whose guidance I conducted my first program evaluations.

Of course, I could not have accomplished this project without the sabbatical funding and support of Loyola College in Maryland, the Maryland Province of the Society of Jesus, and Loyola's education department that enabled me to be away from the classroom for a full year.

Introduction

THE 2006 SEASON of HBO's highly touted but controversial series, *The Wire*, a fictional account of the violent life surrounding the drug trade and neighborhood disintegration in Baltimore, focuses on the lives and struggles of several boys from the urban street corners who are being shortchanged by virtually every institution, including schools, that provide them with few, if any, options for a better life. Ed Burns, a writer and producer of the show, taught in the Baltimore city schools for several years after two decades serving as a city cop. In police work and in teaching, he witnessed firsthand the lessons of violence, mistrust, and disrespect the students learned in their chaotic homes and neighborhoods, lessons that the students would bring with them to school. The series pulled no punches in chronicling the violent behaviors that kids perpetrate against one another when they feel crossed or disrespected along with the failure of urban schools to provide an education that connects to the students' real lives and helps them acquire needed skills for occupational success and personal growth. It would be easy to dismiss HBO's portrayal of urban middle schools as fiction if it were not for the consistent and very real testimonies of children, parents, and teachers about the same deplorable conditions that the show exposed.

Several years ago, when conducting my first examination of the effectiveness of Nativity schools, I visited two urban public middle schools located in the same Baltimore zip codes where students who attended the Nativity schools lived in order to compare the academic and social climate of these schools with that of the new Nativity schools. In one of the public schools, where I observed a far-from-inspiring social studies lesson, the seven sixth-grade boys who participated in a group interview with me spoke about how one of the first tasks they faced as an incoming student was to find someone to physically beat up. This accomplishment afforded them some modicum of safety in the school. They also testified as to the violent peer culture that erupted constantly in hall fights and threats of violence to anyone who did not acquiesce to the demands of physically powerful students to surrender clothing or food or to hook school. In addition, the students noted how teachers tend not to discipline students for misbehavior lest they become victims of student violence. So great were these distractions, as were the ones depicted on *The Wire*, that students were not able to direct much attention to learning regardless of what the teachers had to offer.

The social and learning climate of Nativity schools, which educate children from the same kinds of neighborhoods and backgrounds as the urban public schools, is much more conducive to learning and healthy young adolescent development. The students who attend the Nativity middle schools are able to find a place where people care about them and help them focus their energies on academics and building meaningful and safe relationships, two important domains of young adolescent development.

When I entered Mother Seton Academy, one of Baltimore's first Nativity schools, during my first examination of the Nativity model, I experienced an environment in which children I passed in the hall way stopped to welcome me and shake my hand. In the classrooms I entered, children stood and welcomed me as a group and teachers conducted well-managed classes in which the children were attentive and engaged. In addition, boys and girls attended single-sex classes for academic instruction, thereby eliminating one of the more salient distractions to learning for this raging-hormone age group.

Since that early study, much of my personal and professional interests and concerns have continued to focus on the plight of urban education and the value of the Nativity schools. As a professor at Loyola College, I require my students to spend some time in a Nativity school working with middle school students as tutors, mentors, coaches, or homework helpers. During my 2003–2004 sabbatical year, when I conducted the study of Nativity schools that informs much of this book, I too spent time with some Nativity students as I served as an assistant coach of the lacrosse team at St. Ignatius Loyola Academy in Baltimore. In addition to helping the boys master the difficult skills of passing, catching, and scooping ground balls with a piece of athletic equipment not familiar to most urban children, I experienced the difficult work of the teacher-coach of assisting the boys to understand teamwork and how to react effectively to difficult challenges brought on by physical play and competition. For example, one task was to help them respond to a forceful body block thrown on one of their teammates during a game with something other that the knee-jerk reaction to retaliate with violence. I also learned the importance of maintaining a respectful, caring, and authoritative presence as a teacher and coach if I were to gain and maintain the trust of these students.

Through the service-learning required in my child and adolescent development class, our college students are challenged, in the words of Rev. Peter Hans-Kolvenbach, S. J. (2001), the superior general of the Society of Jesus, to "let the gritty reality of this world into their lives so they can feel it, think about it critically, respond to its suffering, and engage it constructively" (p. 30). By participating in my course and other courses required of our undergraduate elementary education majors, Loyola College students interact with urban children and take part in classroom activities in a Nativity school as well as urban public and parochial Pre–K-to-eighth-grade schools. They learn firsthand that not all children receive the kind of quality education that nearly all of them have come to take for granted. They return from these experiences feeling both discouraged and encouraged, but able to see that the education of urban children placed at risk can be improved and that many urban children are bright and motivated to succeed. Several of them come to care deeply for urban children and are more committed to improving the education these children receive, armed with a social justice framework for understanding the factors contributing to as well as the implications of the failures of American urban public education.

During my sabbatical, when I traveled to seven cities and visited twelve schools that had adopted at least some important elements of the Nativity model, I managed to taste some of the gritty reality of places like Dorchester, Massachusetts, the lower east side of Manhattan, and Anacostia in Washington, DC, areas through which I would not have walked otherwise. I also witnessed effective education taking place in the Nativity schools in these areas where children were thriving and striving for a future they have learned can be available to them. These children were experiencing high levels of self-efficacy and a hope that they could not have imagined a short time earlier. By providing the children with an education that showed them the way to higher educational attainment along with the skills necessary for the journey, Nativity schools have been a living example of a social justice initiative that is making a difference.

My urban and international experiences have gifted me with an increased, albeit insufficient and naive, understanding of the societal conditions that oppress groups of people. I have come to see that education is one of the contexts in which this oppression is carried out against children of color who are banished to neglected urban neighborhoods and schools and made invisible. My experiences also have introduced me to dozens of incredible educators and community leaders of many races and ethnicities who work hard to make the invisible visible and the oppressed educated and supplied with greater social capital. These people in the schools I visited during my sabbatical are true servants—people willing to share their very hearts and souls with children and their parents who are neglected and rejected in today's complex information-driven global economy. I developed a deep respect for these administrators and teachers and their work of taking tangible steps toward helping hundreds of urban children become equipped with educational and social skills to participate meaningfully in an American life among those with power and social and economic capital.

This book reports on a national movement that seeks to raise up children from the bowels of urban decay and provide them with an education that prepares them to gain access to the best institutions of secondary and higher education, to participate in the society with the powerful, and to lead continued efforts to rebuild a society in which power is shared by people of all colors, ethnicities, and social backgrounds. The children who attend Nativity schools enter with very poor reading and math skills but with an unusual opportunity for accelerating their learning and social-emotional development. They leave middle school prepared to succeed in elite private and strong public magnet high schools, with the continued support of the caring people who provided them with a middle school education that matters.

In addition to the research data I collected on Nativity schools and some comparison schools, I attempt to represent the day-to-day operation of the schools that I absorbed from observations and conversations with children, teachers, administrators, graduates, and parents. I hope that these descriptions of the actual experiences of all of these stakeholders tell the inside story of the Nativity model schools.

The "achievement gap" is a term used frequently in reports of the condition of education in the United States. For example, the National Center for Educational Statistics (NCES, 2004a, 2004b) has documented the continued gaps in standardized test score performance in mathematics and reading that leave behind black and Hispanic students. The indicators are particularly deplorable for middle school students. Statistics on science achievement tell the same story (Ruby, 2006). Reasons for these achievement gaps will be explored in chapter 1, along with what research has shown to characterize effective urban middle school education.

The model of Nativity middle school education examined in this study is gaining considerable attention, and momentum, throughout the United States. It is being actualized currently in more than sixty private schools and has been responsible for educating thousands of students placed at risk over the past thirty-seven years. So named for the first of these schools, Nativity Mission Center, which opened in 1971 on the lower east side of Manhattan, Nativity schools are operated by Catholic religious orders as well as by Episcopal and private groups without a religious affiliation. Although the term, Nativity, is used to identify the middle school model examined in this book, the term, NativityMiguel, is more appropriate today with the merging in 2006 of two networks of middle schools based on the Nativity Mission program. All schools that had been part of the Nativity Network and the Lasallian San Miguel Network are now subsumed under the NativityMiguel Network of Schools. The Nativity model and the history of its development is described in detail in chapter 2.

In the examination of the Nativity model that forms the basis of this book, I collected data through classroom observations, interviews, students' standardized test scores, materials published by the schools, and pencil-and-paper questionnaires completed by students, teachers, and administrators at the schools in order to examine the strengths and shortcomings of the model as it is implemented. These data were collected between the summer of 2002 and the summer of 2004 for this evaluation study at eleven such schools that fell under the Nativity banner. Details on the methods of data collection and the materials used are provided in the appendices.

Beginning in chapter 3, I present an analysis of the extensive quantitative and qualitative data collected to illustrate how the Nativity model has been implemented in the eleven middle schools I visited. I report on similarities and differences among the schools with respect to school and class sizes, the length and structure of the school day, the kinds of afternoon and weekend activities offered students, the nature of the teaching staffs and administrative teams, the types of summer programs available, and the nature of the continued support provided to graduates. Here the reader will begin to become acquainted with particular Nativity schools and school personnel.

In chapter 4, I examine the academic indicators of student success in Nativity schools, comparing standardized test scores of Nativity students to those of students in two comparison schools and to published scores of public schools and school districts. High school graduation rates and college matriculation rates are also examined, as are factors that contribute to students' levels of academic engagement and achievement. In addition, I report on an examination of factors that distinguish a high-performing Nativity school with one with less impressive academic outcomes.

I continue the analysis of the success of the Nativity model in chapter 5 by taking a close look at how the schools contribute to their students' social, emotional, moral, and spiritual development, including the development of their leadership skills. These areas form an extremely important aspect of the Nativity mission and reflect a growing concern among educators (see Delpit, 2006b).

In chapter 6, I examine the instructional quality of Nativity schools, especially in light of the use of a considerable number of volunteer teachers. These young adults, who possess educational backgrounds that are quite similar to those selected for the Teach for America program (e.g., strong academic credentials, a desire to make a difference in the lives of children placed at risk, and the personal qualities to succeed in challenging environment), teach classes, tutor children after school, and supervise sports and other activities without a teaching certificate or much, if any, teaching experience. I examine the issue of using volunteer teachers effectively in light of research that questions the educational value of having noncertified and inexperienced teachers and the No Child Left Behind requirements that teachers be highly qualified.

The important issues of educational costs and funding for Nativity schools are addressed in chapter 7. To accomplish the many challenging goals of a Nativity education, costs are bound to be high and the need for effective fund-raising is great. How the Nativity schools decide to spend money to attract funds to the schools is explored here.

The book then closes in chapter 8 with a discussion of the findings I present in light of what research has shown about effective middle school education for urban students at risk and larger issues of social justice in education. Providing a quality education for all children is a matter of social justice, and documents of the Society of Jesus, which is responsible for the operation of approximately twenty of the Nativity schools in existence today, are replete with calls to those educated in the Jesuit tradition to help construct a more just world. I also examine how elements of the Nativity model can be, and are being, adopted effectively in larger educational settings to help meet the overwhelming need for more effective urban education that aims truly at leaving no child behind.

The reader is referred to the appendices for a detailed explanation of the methods of data collection and analysis used in this study. Because all of the schools in the study fell under the umbrella of the Nativity network of schools when most of the data were collected, and did not include any San Miguel schools, I refer to the schools throughout the book as Nativity schools rather than the current designation of NativityMiguel schools.

There is a great deal that educators can learn from the Nativity schools about transforming middle school education for urban children placed at risk. In this closing chapter, I encourage educators to incorporate aspects of the Nativity model in their plans to improve the education of urban children. As *The Wire* episodes pointed out so graphically, too many children continue to be left behind without much hope for a successful and meaningful future. The Nativity schools (now under the umbrella of NativityMiguel schools) provide hope and the skills needed for more of these children to succeed.

ONE

The Current State of
Urban Middle Schools

A RECORD OF FAILURE

THE MARKING OF the fiftieth anniversary of the landmark *Brown v. Board of Education of Topeka, Kansas*, Supreme Court decision in May 2004 has led educators, analysts, politicians, and journalists to closely examine the current state of public education for black and other children of color in the United States. The prevailing view is that *Brown* failed to deliver. The quality of education for children of color continues to be inferior to that afforded most white children. With shameful gaps in achievement test scores continuing, concerned observers are searching for ways to provide all children with equal access to good quality education (e.g., Cose, 2004; Hale, 2001; Hendrie, 2004).

Most of the attention to issues of equal access and the racial gaps in achievement scores has been focused on the American city, in which public schools seem to be in considerable trouble. Noguera (2003) summarized the state of these schools in a single word—*failure*—and indicated that this failure is pervasive. He and others have cited low student achievement and attendance and unmotivated students and teachers among the problems faced by these schools. According to Thernstrom and Thernstrom (2003), many schools, especially those in big cities, have neither adequate building leadership nor a critical mass of good teachers necessary to provide quality educational programs for their children. Lisa Delpit, in the introduction to the 2006 edition of her important work, *Other People's Children: Cultural Conflict in the Classroom*, described how the No Child Left Behind legislation continues to undermine efforts at urban school improvement. In addition, she challenged readers to recognize how the destruction from a hurricane exposed the racism and classism that has continued to keep those who are materially poor and those with dark skin poorly served and neglected.

7

Despite the fifty-five years of the opportunity for reform since *Brown*, the problems of American educational institutions continue to adversely affect non-Asian minority children and adolescents much more so than they affect white children (Thernstrom & Thernstrom, 2003). Even among those with the same level of academic attainment, black and Hispanic students lag behind white and Asian students. Citing National Assessment of Educational Progress (NAEP) test results, Thernstrom and Thernstrom reported that by the twelfth grade black students on the average are four years behind white and Asian students in academic skills, with Hispanic students not faring much better. So dire is this situation that, according to these authors, employers who wish to hire people who are literate and numerate will be hard-pressed to find them among blacks and Hispanics with high school diplomas. In addition, black college graduates tend not to achieve the levels of prose literacy or quantitative literacy that whites do with less than two years of college. Adding to these concerns are the figures for the relatively high dropout rates for Hispanic and African American youth. For example, according to the National Center for Educational Statistics (NCES, 2003), 27 percent of Hispanic sixteen through twenty-four year olds were high school dropouts in 2000, as were 10.9 percent of individuals identified as *Black, non-Hispanic*. Only 7.3 percent of whites and 3.6 percent of Asian/Pacific Islanders in that age group were identified as dropouts. The high dropout rate for Hispanic young adults is explained, in part, by the 43 percent rate among non-English-speaking Hispanic immigrants, more than double that for first- and subsequent-generation Hispanic young adults (15 and 14 percent, respectively). The Alliance for Excellent Education (Joftus, 2002) indicated in its report on the state of secondary education that, while fewer than 75 percent of eighth graders end up graduating from high school in five years, this rate dips to below 50 percent in urban communities.

THE PROBLEM: INEFFECTIVE SCHOOLS AND DISENGAGED STUDENTS

Hale (2001) contended that the schools that most African American children attend—the urban public schools—teach a watered-down curriculum that fails to provide students with the knowledge and skills needed to pass competency exams, achieve in college, or be competitive in the workplace. Limited English-proficient children and adolescents may be at an even greater disadvantage since they are approximately four years behind their peers in reading levels in eighth grade and approximately five years behind in twelfth grade (Alliance for Excellent Education, 2003b). In addition, Greene and Forster (2003), in a working paper prepared for the Manhattan Institute for Policy Research, concluded that the K–12 educational system carries much of the blame for the fact that black and Hispanic students graduate or leave high school qualified to enter college at much lower rates than does the population as a whole.

Two decades ago, the Carnegie Council on Adolescent Development (1989), in its landmark document, *Turning Points*, sounded the alarm that showed that far too many young adolescents were being left behind and ill prepared for a productive future. The council estimated that one-quarter of American adolescents were in "serious jeopardy" with respect to the risks of school failure, substance abuse, and early risky sexual intercourse and reported that the critical reasoning skills of large numbers of young adolescents were "extremely deficient" (p. 27). It declared that a serious mismatch existed between middle schools and the developmental needs of their students and that risks faced by young adolescents are greater for those who are economically poor, members of minority groups, or recent immigrants, in part because these students generally attend the weakest schools.

Certainly, the problem of ineffective urban schooling adversely affects African American and Hispanic children and adolescents most of all and, among them, boys more than girls. In suggesting a model for improving education for African American children, Hale (2001) noted a number of ways in which black adolescents and young adults lag behind their white counterparts in educational and career attainment and called for schools to change the way they educate African American children. Inadequate elementary and secondary education for African American children, designed more for the learning styles of middle-class white children than for children of color, sets in motion a chain of events that threatens the economic and emotional health of the African American family. She contended that African American students tend to attend secondary schools that demand so little that too few of them are able to achieve a passing grade on competency examinations required for high school graduation (see also Alliance for Excellent Education, 2003a). In addition, African American and Hispanic children and adolescents are more likely than white students to be taught by teachers who are inexperienced and poorly prepared (Prince, 2002). Furthermore, according to Hale, African American adolescents who do enter college tend to enroll in two-year rather than four-year institutions, to graduate with a bachelor's degree less often than whites, and to take several more years to complete the baccalaureate.

For a multitude of reasons, economically poor children, especially minority children living in conditions of economic poverty, have a more difficult time persisting through the high school years, much less experiencing the academic success achieved by middle-class and upper-class children (Rist, 2000). Living in urban poverty affects the quality of the education of minority children, in part because of their exposure to continuous and multiple threats to their physical, emotional, and cognitive well-being at home (Evans, 2004), as well as because of the schools' failure to provide adequate support for their academic development. In the introduction written for the republication of his 1970 article on inequities in urban education for the *Harvard Educational Review*, Rist (2000) wrote that very little had changed in thirty years in terms of the extent to which urban schools are ill prepared to meet the needs of the large numbers of black and Hispanic children living in economic poverty.

Identifying the problem of the failure of American educational institutions, particularly those in urban areas, to properly educate the nation's children of color is only one small step in moving toward solving the problem. Jawanza Kunjufu (1989) urged the educational and political communities to spend more time examining causes of the problem and identifying and implementing solutions. Citing the sound educational research of Edmunds, Rist, and others, Kunjufu suggested that the most important factors affecting the low levels of academic achievement of urban children and youth lie within the educational setting and include teachers' low expectations of students' chances for success, the use of tracking, the poor quality of school curricula, bias in testing, and failure to tailor teaching approaches to students' learning styles. He also included peer pressure and low levels of parental involvement as important contributors, along with students' low levels of self-esteem. Less significant, he wrote, are family or neighborhood socioeconomic factors or how many parents the child has in the home, an opinion that also has been expressed by Jencks and Phillips (1998).

Hale (2001) suggested that the root of the problem of schools failing to meet the educational needs of African American children and adolescents lies in their inability to adapt pedagogy and structures to African American culture and the kinds of challenges faced by African American families. Because the majority of African American families are headed by a single parent who has to work longer hours for less pay than whites earn, the structures for involving parents in the schools that work for middle-class white families cannot be applied. Also, because African American children tend to be more kinesthetic than white children in their learning styles and to have a higher level of motor activity, teachers need to adapt learning activities to these characteristics and provide instruction that is "variable, vigorous, and captivating" (p. 117). Since, as she contends, many African American children, especially boys, are not intrinsically interested in school, largely because the curriculum rarely provides a good fit for their learning styles and cultural background, they tend to drop out intellectually by fifth grade and drift along until they can legally extricate themselves from school at age sixteen. So serious is the failure of schools to educate African American boys that she declared the need to improve the outlook for these children as the "most critical issue facing the African American community and American society" (p. 37).

Although the success of Hispanic children in U.S. schools depends in large part on their English language skills, schools could be doing much better to educate children from various Hispanic backgrounds as well (Therstrom & Therstrom, 2003). Factors that provide obstacles to learning for these children include the fact that two-thirds of Latino children in the United States live with parents who are immigrants to the United States and are likely to be uneducated and unskilled, in addition to speaking little or no English. Accounting for one-sixth of the K–12 enrollments, Latino children, the majority of whose families are from Mexico, perform better in school and on standardized tests the longer their families have lived in the United States, although possessing adequate English language skills remains a problem for many third-generation students (Therstrom & Therstrom, 2003). The President's Advisory Commission on Educational Excellence for Hispanic Americans (2003) charged that school personnel must help Hispanic American families understand the school culture for them to help their children succeed academically. The report also cited the low expectations that too many Americans hold for these children as a second obstacle to the academic achievement of Hispanic American children that schools must address. The commission also called for more research to better identify the diverse learning needs of the culturally and linguistically heterogeneous Hispanic American population.

Urban public schools, including middle schools, are beset with numerous problems, including poor-quality instruction, high levels of teacher and student absenteeism, insufficient teaching resources, and lack of professional development and coaching opportunities (Mac Iver, Ruby, Balfanz, & Byrnes, 2003; NCES, 1996). In addition, urban schoolchildren are more than twice as likely to be living at or below the poverty line and, related to the high concentration of low-income students in their schools, to attend schools with levels of student performance lower than in schools in suburban or rural areas (NCES, 1996). Students who attend urban schools are also more likely to be exposed to safety and health risks that mitigate against high levels of academic success (NCES, 1996). These children also tend to spend less time on homework and to watch television more than their suburban or rural counterparts (NCES, 1996).

The debate continues as to how much of an effect living in a low SES environment has on student achievement and whether effective schools and classroom practices can overcome social and economic disadvantage (Trimble, 2004). Surely, children who face the economic poverty, parental unemployment, and community disintegration found in many urban centers are more at risk for school disengagement and failure (George & Alexander, 2003), but such conditions do not render these children unable to learn or succeed. That the problem lies primarily with the schools is further indicated by a report from the Council of Great City Schools (2003) that revealed that more than half of urban schoolchildren attend schools where the per-child expenditures are below the average for their state. In addition, several reports (e.g., Alliance for Excellent Education, 2003a; Prince, 2002) have shown that these same children and adolescents tend to be taught by less qualified and inexperienced teachers who lack adequate instructional support. As reported by the Educational Testing Service (Barton, 2003), more than one-quarter of black and Hispanic eighth graders, and 22 percent of economically poor children in eighth grade, in 2000, were being taught mathematics by teachers who lacked certification in middle level or secondary mathematics. Furthermore, these figures had increased by seven to ten percentage points from 1996 levels.

Yet, as schools struggle under the thumb of the No Child Left Behind requirements for continuous standardized testing, the education of so many of our urban children has become even more formulaic and removed from the real lives of children. As Delpit (2006b) pointed out, today's education continues to leave children unchallenged and to ignore the development of their character.

A SOLUTION: EFFECTIVE MIDDLE SCHOOLS

Despite the ills of urban public schooling and the risks faced by students who live with social and economic disadvantage, several recent efforts have shown that children and adolescents of color who attend some urban public and private schools, including those with high concentrations of low-income students, can and do experience educational success. Two successful urban middle school efforts include KIPP (Knowledge Is Power Program; Thernstrom & Thernstrom, 2003) and Talent Development middle schools (Mac Iver et al., 2003; Norton, 2000). Common elements of these two models include the use of research and standards-based instructional programs, extra help sessions, a longer period for English instruction, a supportive learning environment, and student leadership development. Teacher development aimed at equipping teachers with classroom management and instructional skills appropriate for the middle school children they encounter is a key feature of the Talent Development model (Mac Iver et al., 2003). In KIPP schools, the principal, who has attended an intensive training session by KIPP directors, along with teachers set high expectations for student effort, achievement, and behavior. Instruction is of a high caliber and parents and students sign a contract to express their commitment to the demands of the KIPP school (Thernstrom & Thernstrom, 2003). On my visit to KIPP Ujima Village Academy in Baltimore, I observed an orderly environment in which student time on task was high and behavior problems virtually nonexistent.

These school programs seem to put into action, with excellent results, the characteristics of effective middle schools that have been described in various research and research-based publications (e.g., George & Alexander, 2003; Lipsitz, 1984; Trimble, 2004). As George and Alexander (2003) and others have pointed out, effective middle schools provide an environment that matches, or fits with, young adolescents' developmental needs. Lewis (2000) summarized these characteristics as follows:

1. The establishment of small communities for learning that include inter-disciplinary teaching teams, a common planning time for teachers on the team, and teacher-led advisories for students.
2. A curriculum in core courses and the use of teaching and learning activities that are engaging, developmentally appropriate, and challenging for all students so as to maximize student learning.
3. Parent contact about individual student performance and information sharing with parents that encourages meaningful parent involvement in the school.
4. A school environment that values mutual respect and care and that also holds students and teachers to high behavioral expectations.
5. High-quality ongoing training for teachers in teaching techniques and interdisciplinary team functioning that will ensure a program that meets the developmental needs of the students and provides them with the challenge and support needed for them to succeed.

These very themes were endorsed in the 1989 publication of *Turning Points*. In addition, the *Turning Points* report called for alternative instructional strategies that involved the elimination of tracking and the use of cooperative learning, the promotion of health and fitness, and the establishment of collaborations within the community within which the school is located. In addition, Bradford (1999) called for teachers, especially those of minority middle school students, to guide student learning in ways that were authentic and meaningful to students and that met their individual learning needs. With respect to teacher qualities, Delpit (2006b) has emphasized the need for teachers of children of color to be direct and authoritative—that is, to take charge in the classroom, command student respect, and push students to achieve. Furthermore, Noguera (2003) found that schools that are successful in educating economically poor children are those that are guided by a coherent mission that is embraced by administrators, teachers, students, and parents.

A research summary on factors that improve student achievement published by the National Middle School Association (Trimble, 2004) provides more detail on the characteristics of effective middle level education. For example, the report detailed several classroom practices that have been empirically documented to improve student learning, including establishing a classroom climate that was task-oriented, which involves focusing instruction on targeted outcomes, setting learning goals based on standards, and conducting periodic assessments of learning. With respect to effective teaching strategies,

Trimble addressed the importance of teachers setting high standards, along with being willing to give students the assistance they need to achieve, promoting higher order and critical thinking, promoting student engagement in the learning process, and providing students with meaningful learning tasks in an integrated curriculum. Also, enhancement of the curriculum in mathematics and language arts, particularly with respect to reading and writing, and offering students with extra support when needed have been identified in research as related to higher levels of student achievement. Trimble also underscored the need for teachers to be well trained and talented classroom leaders and for principals to be strong leaders who place a high value on student learning, effective instruction, and teacher support. Along with maintaining a strong academic focus, teachers and principals need to be caring individuals genuinely committed to the students. Not to be forgotten, George and Alexander (2003) underscored the need for middle school students to feel known and cared for.

Information provided directly by urban students underscores the importance of much of what the research data tell us. Having conducted interviews with over 360 middle school students from among the poorest neighborhoods and lowest performing middle schools in Philadelphia, Wilson and Corbett (2001) reported several consistent themes in students' reports. For example, they reported that students overwhelmingly preferred teachers who were strict but respectful, who explained material clearly and in multiple ways when necessary, and who were eager to help students, but not play favorites. The students felt that teachers needed to stay on the children who stepped out of line, address misbehavior strictly and fairly, continually motivate them to learn, and explain material to them in ways that they can understand.

The Nativity model schools included in the present study are examined in light of the qualities deemed important for effective middle schools, in particular urban middle schools that educate children of color. I collected considerable data, both quantitative and qualitative, from students, teachers, administrators, alumni, and parents. Variations in the extent of the schools' incorporation of the qualities associated with effective middle school education are presented along with the implications of these variations for student achievement and development. First, I will describe the Nativity model and the history behind its development.

TWO

The Nativity School Model

NATIVITY HISTORY

THE FIRST NATIVITY model school, which opened as a middle school in the fall of 1971, grew out of a program operated by a group of Catholic nuns who were working to meet the social, recreational, and spiritual needs of the children of immigrants from Puerto Rico who moved into the lower east side of Manhattan after World War II to work in the factories of the thriving garment industry. When a Jesuit priest, Reverend Walter Janer, S.J., arrived at the Nativity Mission Center in the mid-1950s, the center took on a strong academic focus; neighborhood children came for tutoring, in addition to the other programs. The tutoring program expanded to a summer experience in the early 1960s at Camp Monserrate to continue the educational mission of the center.

In the midst of an atmosphere of social decay in the lower east side in the 1960s, Nativity Mission Center continued to offer after-school and evening programs for the Puerto Rican and other youth of the neighborhood. Under the leadership of Fr. Gene Feeney, S.J., and with the inspiration of lay collaborator, Michael Mincieli, an evaluation began in the late 1960s of the effectiveness of the center's mission and programs, the needs of the young people of the community, and the charism of the Jesuit order. A central question that was addressed was whether the programs of the center contributed to true systemic change or provided a temporary band-aid to the problems brought on by the severe economic poverty of the area. Subsequently, in 1971, the decision was made to focus the center's activities around a middle school for boys in grades six through eight. Mike Mincieli became its first principal. Boys returning from Camp Monserrate that summer were instructed to appear at Nativity Mission Center by 8 A.M. on September 13 to begin classes in the new Nativity Mission Center School.

This chapter is coauthored by Rev. John J. Podsiadlo, S.J.

Throughout the 1970s and 1980s, Nativity was a unique program for Latino boys placed at risk because of economic poverty. As the first middle school operated by the Society of Jesus, Nativity was not tuition-driven since the families paid next to nothing and fund-raising was its only means of support. A core staff of Jesuits and volunteers lived on the top floor of the five-story tenement building. After a day of rigorous classes, especially in reading, writing, grammar, spelling, math, and science, the boys would spend several hours in sports, clubs, or tutoring before going home for dinner. It was common for them to be confronted on the walk home by members of a local gang with comments about the single-sex school they attended or the number of books they were carrying. At 7 P.M. the boys returned to the school for evening study, after which a teacher would drive them home through the drug-infested streets of the neighborhood. From those first classes, several "made it" to prestigious parochial high schools. Others attended public high school and then joined the military and a few succumbed to the lure of the streets, while two went on to prestigious colleges such as Cornell University.

The first twenty-five years of the Nativity Mission Center middle school program saw the leadership of some devoted educators. One man, Mike Mincieli, who started working at the center as a high school student in the mid-1960s and later was involved in starting the middle school program, lived and worked at the school, as well as the center prior to the opening of the school, for over twenty-five years. He was also instrumental in setting the tone of the school and summer camp, which he also directed for twenty years. In addition, Fr. Jack Podsiadlo, S. J., the coauthor of this chapter, returned to the school in 1984 as principal and executive director, after having taught at the school from 1973 through 1979. Fr. Jack helped to establish structures to improve accounting and fund-raising practices, especially with foundations, aligned the curriculum to state and archdiocese standards, and put into place a mentor teacher and young teacher development program to improve the instructional quality of the classes. He also helped formalize the graduate support program that expanded its high school placements to out-of-town boarding schools and prepared graduates in high school for college application and admission.

By the late 1980s, the successful Nativity Mission Center school was gaining notice and Nativity personnel became instrumental in forming new Nativity model schools. The second Nativity school, Nativity Preparatory School, opened in Boston in 1990 under the leadership of a University of Notre Dame graduate, who taught at Nativity Mission and obtained the support of the New England Province of Jesuits to sponsor the school. One of the Jesuits who helped start the Nativity Mission Center middle school founded the third Nativity model school in Harlem in 1991. Both schools admitted only boys.

Soon members of other Catholic religious congregations began to visit the flagship school. Visits led to planning and planning to openings, many of which took place in 1993, including two schools for girls—Mother Caroline

Academy and Education Center in Roxbury, Massachusetts, and Cornelia Middle School of the Holy Child, just a short walk from the original Nativity school. Mother Seton Academy was founded in Baltimore that same year by six religious congregations to educate both boys and girls but in single-gender classes. Also in 1993, the Jesuits opened two schools for boys, St. Ignatius Loyola Academy in Baltimore and Nativity Jesuit Middle School in Milwaukee, and the De LaSalle Christian Brothers opened San Miguel school in Providence, Rhode Island. Based in large part on the Nativity model, San Miguel School of Providence was the first of over a dozen middle school initiatives for the Christian Brothers that later fell under the umbrella of the NativityMiguel Network of Schools. Since then, at least one new school opened nearly every year through 2006. Although no new schools opened in 2007, two new schools were expected to open in the fall of 2008. The faces of the sponsoring organizations became more varied also, as Catholic support broadened to lay boards and Episcopal sponsorships. The Epiphany School sponsored by the Episcopal Diocese of Boston opened in 1997 as did Academy Prep Center of St. Petersburg, Florida, sponsored by a lay board of directors that planned to sponsor three additional Nativity schools in Florida. By the end of 2006, there were over thirty different religious congregations, dioceses, or lay boards sponsoring forty-four Nativity model middle schools across the United States, with the Society of Jesus continuing to sponsor approximately one-half of the Nativity schools. (Some Nativity schools are sponsored by several different religious congregations.) Twenty-seven schools were opened between 2001 and 2006, a growth due in part to funding provided to schools by the Cassin Educational Initiative Foundation for planning and start-up costs.

As the number of Nativity and Lasalian San Miguel schools grew, representatives of the administrations of the schools began to meet to discuss a host of issues including the Nativity mission, curriculum and planning, fundraising, teacher recruitment and development, and summer programs. Annual meetings in the late 1990s led to the formation of a national network to coordinate training efforts and fund-raising activities. The Nativity Educational Centers Network was formed in 2001 with its office in Baltimore headed by Fr. Jack Podsiadlo, S.J., the long-time director of the Nativity Mission School in New York. Supported by the Cassin Educational Initiative Foundation, the Foundation for Nativity and Miguel Schools was formed in 2003 with the purpose of furthering the work of the Nativity and Lasallian San Miguel networks that together educated over four thousand middle school students in eighteen states at that time.

During the years 2001 to 2006, a series of gatherings or institutes were inaugurated to support the key staff members and further the communicating and networking among the schools. Supported by funds from several foundations and private donors, annual workshops or institutes are held each year, or nearly every year, for principals, development directors and presidents, graduate support directors, and teachers. Best practices are shared and workshops are presented that help ensure educational quality in the schools.

What from 1971 through 1989 was a single school has expanded over the next nineteen years into a network of sixty-four schools spread across twenty-seven states and educating thousands of underserved middle school boys and girls from low-income families. These schools continue to support their graduates both programmatically and financially through high school and into college, thus partnering with them and their families in their efforts to break the cycle of poverty through education. Graduates of some of the older schools are returning to their alma maters as teachers, graduate support directors, and even board members, giving to a new generation what they so lavishly received. Throughout these years of numerical growth, the goal of the national leadership has been to ensure that the essential elements of the successful model remain constant. The sustainability of the existing schools along with creating new schools form the goals for the future of the NativityMiguel Network.

THE NATIVITY MODEL

Defining features of the Nativity model, now promoted as common elements of NativityMiguel middle schools, include:

- small class size and small school communities
- extended day and year
- faith-based program
- service to the economically poor and marginalized
- partnership with the family
- graduate mentoring and college counseling
- a holistic education (NativityMiguel Network of Schools, n.d., Overview)

The small school and class size and a small student–teacher ratio allow for personal mentoring and intensive academic work. Data provided by the NativityMiguel Network (2007) show an average school size of seventy-three and an average of eighteen students per grade. In addition, the schools employ an average of six full-time salaried and seven full-time volunteer faculty members, or fewer than six faculty members per student. These data also show that approximately 96 percent of schools provide a summer program of some sort that takes place for two weeks or more. These programs tend to combine continued academic skill development with leadership, spiritual, and social skill development. The NativityMiguel Network (2007) also reports an average school day of nine hours that includes homework help and tutoring sessions staffed by volunteer teachers and community volunteers.

Nativity schools also have varied in their approaches to admitting students into their school programs. In the first few years of operation, most schools admitted almost every child who applied and who also qualified with respect to household income in order to fill their classes, a situation that changed once the word spread about the quality of the schools, as well as their low cost. When the number of applications exceeded the number of available slots, each of the schools had to determine criteria for selection that enabled them to remain true to their mission of educating children from low-income homes who were not being served well in their public schools.

Nativity schools continue to offer academic, social, emotional, and financial support to their graduates throughout their high school years, and even into their college years, through their graduate support program (GSP). The GSP director also provides support and services for graduates and their families to help them obtain college admission and financial aid. Podsiadlo and Philliber (2003) viewed the services of the graduate support program at Nativity Mission as a strong contributor to the relatively high rates of high school completion, college entry, and college graduation for its graduates.

Because all of the Nativity schools are private and require parents to pay at most a small tuition or fee, funding is a significant concern. The small fees paid by families help to solidify parents' levels of commitment to their children's education, but contribute very little to the operating costs (Podsiadlo & Philliber, 2003).

Nativity schools expend considerable effort and expense to raise much-needed student scholarship funds from private donors and to secure the support of individuals, foundations, and public granting agencies for curricular, cocurricular, after-school, summer, and other school programs. Because of the importance of fund-raising, many Nativity schools employ a leadership structure of a principal, with primary responsibility for directing the educational program, and a president or executive director who works closely with members of the board of trustees to represent the school to the local community and develop contacts with potential supporters. Most boards are composed of educators and community and business leaders. Many of the schools also employ at least one full-time administrator to direct development activities.

Although the first Nativity schools were formed from the founders' assessments of the needs of the families and children in their communities, rather than from the scant literature on effective middle level schools at the time, the schools came to embody much of what came to be known about effective middle level education and effective education for urban children. The most notable characteristics of the Nativity model that are found in the effective middle schools literature include their 6–8 and 5–8 grade-level arrangements, their creation of small classes and communities for learning, the involvement of students' families in the educational enterprise, the emphasis placed on improving skills in reading, writing, and mathematics, and their strong and caring school leadership (George & Alexander, 1993; Jackson & Davis, 2000).

Important to acknowledge in the description of the Nativity and San Miguel schools is the fundamental role that social justice plays in the mission and operation of the schools. The children served in these schools are truly among those to whom public education has provided little. Indeed, they are among the children failed by the public schools in the nation's cities, children from families who possess very little social capital or respect from public school administrators (Noguera, 2003).

The social justice mission of Nativity model schools is consistent with official Jesuit documents that speak strongly about the mandate to work for justice and in solidarity with those people who are economically poor and disenfranchised in society. For example, Decree 3 of the 34th General Congregation (GC 34) of the Society of Jesus (1994–95), on the Jesuit mission and justice, called for a renewed commitment to the work of justice as an integral part of the mission of the Society and the faith of its members. GC 34 acknowledges the important work of the Society and its lay collaborators of educating children and adults who are economically poor, suggesting that such endeavors can be among the most effective of the services the Society can provide people. (See Decree 18 on education.) A similar mandate to educate members of society who are marginalized is found in the documents of other religious groups who are invested in Nativity model schools (e.g., Society of the Holy Child Jesus, 2002).

THE SCHOOLS IN THE PRESENT STUDY

The eleven schools chosen for the present study include five single-sex schools for boys, four operated by the Society of Jesus and one by the Society of St. Edmund, three single-sex schools for girls operated by communities of religious women, including the Society of the Holy Child Jesus and the School Sisters of Notre Dame, and three schools that enroll both boys and girls. One of the coeducational schools is operated by a group of women and men from six different religious communities, one is affiliated with the Episcopal church, and one has no religious affiliation. Schools were chosen for this study in such a way as to ensure a high amount of racial-ethnic variation among the students, a variety of urban locations, and differences in a number of other features including the religious affiliation, if any, of the founders of the schools.

More information on the Nativity schools and their students, as well as two comparison parochial schools and their students, is provided in Appendix A. In addition, the methods used to collect data, which involved school visits, interviews, classroom observations, and surveys completed by students, teachers, and administrators, are described in considerable detail in Appendix B.

THREE

Nativity School
Structures and Programs

THE OLDEST OF THE Nativity model schools is Nativity Mission Center located in the lower east side of Manhattan across from a small park and a few steps below Houston Street. It began its middle school program in 1971 and educates approximately sixty boys in a narrow four-story row house. Having provided tutoring for neighborhood Latino boys through its family mission center prior to its opening as a middle school, the school established the model of small classes for instruction and extended day homework assistance and tutoring. It started its summer camp leadership experience when a generous donor extended an invitation to the school to utilize his camp property near Lake Placid, New York. Pride at being a member of the Nativity Mission fraternity is evident on the faces of the boys and the energy exuded by the students is captivating. I was amazed at how much was being accomplished inside this small building.

What has become known as the Nativity model of middle school education for children placed at risk has its roots in the structure and function of the Nativity Mission Center. This chapter addresses the extent to which the model is realized in eleven Nativity middle schools and how aspects of the school structures and programs in Nativity schools are consistent and differ across the eleven schools included in this study. While certain features of the model are quite consistent, there are some differences that will be identified. Also, in addition to describing the components of the model, I show how administrators and teachers contribute to the unique ways in which the model is brought to life in the schools.

SCHOOL AND CLASS SIZE

One of the defining features of the Nativity schools is the small size of the student body and small class sizes for instruction. For the eleven schools included in this study, there was a mean of 18.2 students per grade, with a range of 9 (one fifth-grade class in a grade 5–8 school) to 26 students. Within each school, the class size for instruction varied from 1 (for pullout instruction in reading) to 16 and the student–teacher ratio averaged an impressive 5.8-to-1.

School size is constrained to a great extent by the size of the facility available to house the school. However, even as some schools have moved out of their initial small quarters, typically an urban row house or church annex, their new or renovated buildings have continued to be designed for the small school sizes befitting the Nativity model. For example, two of the Boston area schools built new school buildings and one purchased and renovated an existing structure after their schools had been in operation for a few years, but all three continued to keep school and class sizes within the structure of the model. The two largest schools in the study educate both girls and boys in grades 5 through 8 and the largest single-sex school enrolled seventy-five boys. The school with the largest enrollment limits the size of each grade, and each class for instruction, to fifteen students and segregates the nearly one hundred boys and girls in separate buildings for the majority of the school day.

Consistent with the literature on effective middle school environments, the small size of the schools and classes contributes considerably to the students' experience of being known by teachers and other students and of being part of a community. In contrast to the sense of anonymity that students often experience in larger urban middle schools (see Simmons & Blyth, 1987), Nativity school students relish the extent to which they are able to form relationships with teachers and students from their own grade, as well as other grades. In my interviews with them at their high school, several graduates of one of the Baltimore schools recalled how the small size of the school proved to be very beneficial with respect to getting to know teachers and students and helping them stay focused on learning. Also, it was common for students to use the terms *family* and *community* when describing their schools. As the findings presented in chapter 4 show, school size is a significant contributor to the supportive climate and extraordinary student academic achievement in Nativity schools.

THE PEOPLE

At the heart of all of the Nativity schools are administrators and teachers who are committed—to the children and families they support and to providing the best education possible. These people are agents of social justice at work who put in long hours of loving service to children who are among those who have been left behind in the urban educational system.

ADMINISTRATORS

The administrative teams of nearly all of the Nativity schools in this study include a president or executive director, a principal or school head who is the academic leader, a director of development, and graduate support program director. Some of the Nativity schools also employ part-time personnel in positions such as a summer camp director and a volunteer coordinator, who organizes and schedules large numbers of volunteer tutors, homework helpers, and mentors. Although having at least four administrators on staff seems excessive for the size of the Nativity schools, the nature of the program and the need to raise a significant amount of funds every year necessitate such a structure and commitment. Other parochial schools, such as the two included in this study for comparison purposes, employ no more than a principal and a vice principal for their administrative teams and do not encounter the levels of per pupil costs that the more extensive Nativity school programs do.

The president or executive director is responsible for the most part for representing the school to the community, serving as the liaison between the school and its board of trustees, and showcasing the school to potential donors. In many, but not all, cases, presidents do not have a great deal of contact with the students themselves, although they all spend some portion of their time at the schools, and only a few maintained their offices in the school building. The president of the Milwaukee school, a Jesuit priest, was unusual in that he taught a weekly course to each class on social and spiritual development issues related to the boys' life challenges and was very involved in the daily life of the school.

Among the eleven schools included in this study, seven of the presidents were members of a sponsoring religions congregation and one was a former religious. Several of the presidents had strong ties to the community that they had developed over a number of years, with a few presidents having ten or more years of involvement with their schools. These individuals were particularly strong assets to their schools in raising funds and increasing resources, such as computer equipment and networking capabilities, and building projects, including housing for volunteer teachers.

In two cases, the president of the Nativity Mission School and the executive director of Academy Prep Center of St. Petersburg oversaw the operation of more than one Nativity school. In addition, the development office staffs located at these two schools served more than one school. Mother Caroline Academy and Education Center in Boston is also unique in its administrative structure in that its executive director oversees an adult education program that includes some of the parents of the school students and an after-school program for third and fourth graders, in addition to the school program. Mother Caroline also has a vice principal on staff who oversees admissions and summer camp placements and three members of its administrative team are also members of a religious community of women. This example shows how a few Nativity schools adopt the model within a larger structure that provides additional services to the community that complemented the goals of the schools.

Principals are extremely active in day-to-day operations of the schools, addressing problems that arise and leading efforts to establish and revise the curriculum and hire qualified faculty. In some schools, the principals have been teachers at the school and many teach a small number of classes. Such is the case at Nativity Mission Center where the principal assumed the leadership of the school after four years of teaching, the first two of which he served as a volunteer teacher. Other schools have hired academic leaders from outside the Nativity network. One of these hires is the headmistress at the New York school for girls who has an advanced degree from a highly regarded graduate program and brought with her a strong background in curriculum development and planning. She also has proved to be a valuable asset to the network of NativityMiguel schools by sharing her expertise through the annual workshops sponsored by the network.

At nearly all the schools included in this study, the academic leader was an experienced educator with considerable experience working in urban educational settings and a strong commitment to the Nativity model. One Nativity headmistress is a veteran of thirty years in Washington, DC, public schools who was attracted to the mission of Nativity schools and became a founding member of her school. An African American woman with strong ties to the city, she is particularly effective at mobilizing community resources and involving parents in the life of the school. She has organized programs for parents to help them better support the educational and social developmental needs of their children and has involved mothers and daughters together in cultural events in the city. At the same time, the headmistress communicates a clear message to the students about their intrinsic value and the importance of a good education. In addition, she was responsible for the creation of a youth chapter at the school of the National Council of Negro Women. The girls respond very positively to her and reported in interviews that they often go to talk with her about their concerns and the life difficulties they face.

The position of graduate support program (GSP) director sets Nativity schools apart from virtually all other programs serving urban children placed at risk. The GSP director helps students and their parents with high school admissions and financial aid applications, schedules events for alumni, maintains personal contact with each graduate, and obtains information from high school guidance counselors on the graduates' performances. The GSP director also arranges tutoring for graduates who require it, helps graduates and their families with college admission applications, and accompanies them on college visits. Most GSP directors also teach at least one class that enables them to get to know the students while they are still in middle school and work to develop relationships with private schools, including boarding schools, that could serve as placements for their graduates. Many of these tasks tend to be taken on by the principal or other administrator in the early years of a school program and to become more formalized once one or more classes of students are enrolled in high school and the task of monitoring students' progress takes up more and more of the administrator's time.

One of the very busy and effective GSP directors is Larry Siewert of the Nativity Jesuit Middle School in Milwaukee, a school he helped to establish with the long-time president and close friend, Rev. Bill Johnson, S.J., in 1993. Bill recruited Larry from his principal's position at a local Catholic high school to serve as the first principal of the new middle school, a post he held for six years and a position that also included assisting Nativity's graduates. No longer principal, Mr. Siewert directs the mentoring program in which each graduate is paired with an individual or couple from the community, sees to it that all mentors receive the students' high school report card grades, oversees the program that provides all graduates with computers, visits the graduates and their counselors weekly in their high schools, and holds regular parent meetings, in addition to all the other tasks of helping to keep graduates on track for high school success. As is the case in several Nativity schools, he also teaches two classes a day and assists with development activities that benefit the school because of his strong ties to the Milwaukee Catholic community.

The development function in each of the schools is extremely important since the schools need to raise funds to cover nearly the entire program budget each year. Because the schools charge little or no tuition (small fees are required in most schools to cover books and other materials), funds must be solicited from private donors and foundations by experienced development personnel. Because the program for one Boston school for eighty students (20 percent of whom are in the foster-care system) offers extensive medical and psychological services, as well as a high-quality education, it employs two professionals in its development office to raise the more than $19,000 per student needed annually. The schools do vary somewhat in the comprehensiveness of their development functions, with a small number of schools conducting little more that regular mass-mailing campaigns. More analysis of the development function appears in chapter 7.

The extent to which a school employs someone in each of these positions, and whether some administrators are employed full time or part time, depends on funding, the size of the school program, and the perceived need to have a person in each position. In some cases, some of the administrative positions, most often the president or executive director, are filled by members of religious communities that donate the administrator's salary and supply living expenses. Such arrangements help to reduce the amount of funds needed to be raised, although the likelihood of schools being able to continue to have religious community members on staff is growing smaller with the declining numbers of men and women in religious life.

TEACHING STAFFS

Nativity school administrators acknowledge the importance of having high-quality instruction that requires the hiring of a competent and effective teaching staff. An interesting characteristic of Nativity schools is that all of them hire at least a small number of volunteer or intern teachers through national organizations, such as Americorps, Jesuit Volunteer Corps (JVC), and Mercy Corps, as well as through local recruiting efforts. The volunteers, who are college graduates with a heart for teaching urban children, usually lack certification and classroom teaching experience. I examine the effectiveness of having these teachers on staff who commit to two or three years to teaching at the school in chapter 6. Here I will address similarities and differences among Nativity schools in their use of volunteer and experienced, certified teachers. The use of volunteer teachers is one area in which considerable variation among Nativity schools exists.

Volunteer teachers have been a vital part of the Nativity landscape since the founding of the Nativity Mission Center school when funds were simply not available to hire a full experienced and certified teaching staff, a situation most of the Nativity schools face today as well. Volunteer teachers receive a small living allowance and are furnished with housing, usually with other volunteers, and receive some additional benefits, such as medical insurance and Americorps educational stipends. They are recruited from among some of the top colleges and universities in the United States and are hired to teach primarily in the content area that corresponds to their college major.

The mean size of the volunteer teaching staff for the eleven Nativity schools included in this study was 5.3 teachers, which represented 46 percent of the instructional staff (a mean of 11.4 FTE teachers). The Boston area boys' school and girls' school topped the list with 71 and 70 percent of the staff, respectively, composed of noncertified volunteer teachers. At the other end of the spectrum, the Washington Middle School for Girls employed only one volunteer teacher (13 percent of the staff) through the Americorps program (see Table A.2).

Volunteer teachers are used in a variety of ways in the Nativity schools. For the most part, the first-year volunteers teach fewer classes per week when compared to second-year volunteer and experienced teachers. However, there is considerable variation in the number of classes they teach and the kinds of duties assigned to them. At Nativity Preparatory School in Boston, for example, first-year volunteers usually teach three classes a day and have four periods available for planning, subject-area team and grade-level meetings, and consultations with the principal or experienced master teachers. Volunteers, who may team teach some classes initially, also have recess and after-school sport or other activity supervisory duties. At the coeducational Boston school, first- and second-year volunteer teachers teach two classes daily, coach a sport, supervise evening dinner and study hall two nights a week, and serve in a leadership role on a school committee. At St. Ignatius Loyola Academy for boys in Baltimore, first-year volunteers teach ten to twelve classes a week and those in their second year teach twelve to fourteen classes. They also lead an advisory group of students and supervise afternoon activities or coach sports teams as well as an evening or Saturday study session each week.

At one end of the spectrum of volunteer teacher use are two schools that employed just one volunteer teacher through Americorps. For example, the volunteer at Mother Seton Academy in Baltimore taught art classes and provided instructional support in and out of the classroom, sometimes serving as classroom aide to support particular students. The Americorps volunteer at Washington Middle School for Girls, on the other hand, taught four classes a day, four days a week. Unlike the situation at schools where a number of volunteers are housed together, Americorps volunteers live with other Americorps volunteers who work in different schools or other kinds of service placements.

Nativity schools are also committed to hiring a core of highly qualified certified teachers, some of whom have considerable experience teaching at area public and parochial schools, although the practice puts more of a strain on budgets than the hiring of volunteer teachers. The certified teachers provide important instructional leadership in the schools and serve as mentors for the volunteer teachers.

COMMUNITY VOLUNTEERS

An important finding of this study is that volunteers from the community contribute substantially to the education of Nativity school students. These volunteers include local high school and college students, as well as older adults—including some with teaching experience. Many serve as homework helpers, who work with the students in the afternoon and evening study halls to help them address any difficulties they encounter on their assignments. Other volunteers serve as tutors who work one-on-one or in small groups with struggling students during the school day or evening study hours.

Volunteers also work with the Nativity students in sports and recreation activities and others serve as mentors who accompany the students on field trips and develop a one-on-one relationship with a student for the purpose of meeting some of the social developmental needs of the students. In the schools I visited, volunteers could be found also supervising the library, providing office support, and assisting accounting and development operations. One Nativity school was fortunate to have a volunteer director of the graduate support program for several years. Of course, all Nativity schools have a number of volunteers serving on their boards of trustees. The description of the services provided by volunteers at the coeducational Nativity school in Baltimore found on the school's Web site illustrates the myriad ways in which community volunteers support the school:

> In addition to part and full-time paid staff members, over 50 volunteers currently share their time, energy, and experience on a weekly basis with Academy students each year. Volunteers from local high schools and colleges as well as working professionals from the area participate in the Academy program as tutors, homework companions, art teachers, a nurse, and maintenance personnel. In addition, volunteers assist as guest speakers, special topic workshop presenters, substitute teachers, etc. Volunteers are a highly-valued, essential aspect of the Academy program. (Mother Seton Academy, 2005)

WITHIN-SCHOOL COLLABORATION

Particularly in Nativity schools with relatively new school buildings, space is provided for teachers to collaborate and support one another's development as effective instructors. In all three of the Boson area schools included in this study, generous areas are set aside where teachers share offices large enough to provide them with opportunities for collegial discussions and team planning. Within these spaces, either the principal (as is the case in the Boston boys' school) or master teachers, or both, are readily available for consultation. In the Boston school for boys, classes are scheduled so that teachers who teach the same subject have the same time slots set aside for team meetings and collaborative planning. Schools also have in place a system of mentoring by experienced teachers that helps to support the development of the inexperienced teachers, although I found a degree of variation in the extent to which inexperienced teachers took advantage of these mentoring programs.

PROFESSIONAL CONSULTANTS

Nearly all Nativity schools are able to secure the services of paid and volunteer professional consultants to support teacher preparation and development. In several schools, for example, local mental health workers or educational consultants are brought in during the school year to provide a forum for teachers to discuss classroom management challenges they face and explore and develop more effective methods of teaching in their content areas. The schools also employ the services of university teacher educators and other educational consultants to help conduct training workshops for inexperienced teachers prior to the start of the school year and follow-up classroom observations and consultations for these teachers.

THE CURRICULUM

For the most part, I found the curriculum at the Nativity schools to be strong in some areas and "developing" in others. Principals and other school leaders indicated that they were most pleased with the status of their reading and language arts programs. Across the board, they viewed these programs as most essential, given the poor performances of most of their incoming students on standardized tests of reading achievement and the lack of adult speakers of English in the homes of children of immigrant families. I found that schools devoted much of the school day to the development of reading and writing skills, including reading fluency and comprehension, spelling, and grammar.

According to a number of school heads with whom I spoke, the schools have undertaken a systematic approach to strengthening the curriculum one content area at a time. This approach seems to be coinciding with the schools' hiring of educational leaders with more of a background in curriculum than may have been the case for some of their predecessors. Nearly all the Nativity schools I visited were either accredited by the regional independent schools association or in the process of seeking such accreditation, and all schools followed the curriculum set forth by the regional diocese or archdiocese or of the state.

To enhance students' reading abilities and to instill a love of reading, many schools have adopted programs such as D.E.A.R., or Drop Everything And Read, in which twenty minutes is set aside each day, or most days, in the school schedule to read independently a book chosen by the student with the help of the language arts teacher. Several schools also take part in the Accelerated Reader (Renaissance Learning, 2006) program that provides computerized quizzes for students to take on completion of a book to assess their comprehension. Teachers keep track of students' progress as they read and help students choose books that challenge as well as interest them. Schools that have not adopted the Accelerated Reader program have structured a reading curriculum that emphasizes the reading of young adult fiction and allows for students to choose some of the books they read. A student at one of the Nativity schools expressed pride in the fact that she was able to read and enjoy reading "more complex" books as an eighth grader. A few Nativity schools also employ a full- or part-time reading specialist who supports classroom teachers and pulls students out who require special assistance. Most schools without a reading specialist have one on their wish list.

The mathematics curriculum appears to be very strong in some schools and on the list for further development in others. All schools used trade books for mathematics instruction that were fairly current and the quality of math instruction was strong in the schools I visited, with many setting aside more than five regular class periods a week for math. In one math class, an experienced teacher was using the overhead projector effectively to instruct eighth graders in an algebraic graphing exercise that was challenging and in which the students were attentive and involved at their desks. Unfortunately, only a few schools were equipped with hands-on materials, or manipulatives, for students to explore math concepts.

The three Boston area Nativity schools I visited took an innovative approach to their science curriculum, with plans to expand the effort to mathematics. The trio of schools together employed a science coordinator to oversee the science program that was funded by the National Science Foundation (NSF). The coordinator helped to train new faculty in the use of the materials provided by NSF for conducting labs and other lessons. I observed one science class in which students worked in groups of three to assess the density of three irregular solids. Each group received a kit containing the solids and materials for measuring weight and displaced volume and for recording data and computing densities. My review of the curriculum for the sixth, seventh, and eighth grades revealed strong science content and excellent materials and readings for students' understanding. Other schools in the Nativity network were not as fortunate to have such materials at their disposal; some even lacked lab space for science and had to address science content in regular classrooms.

I observed effective lessons in social studies, religion, and "life" topics at the Nativity schools that used current texts. Some schools had clearly developed strong curriculums in social studies and many also coordinated social studies units with language arts. All of the schools recognized the importance of helping the students with challenging life decisions, especially with respect to alcohol and other drug use, sexual attitudes and behaviors, and resolving conflict, given the troubled families and dangerous neighborhoods in which most of the children lived.

Many of the schools also included Spanish in their curriculum and one school included Latin in its sixth-grade curriculum. Even in the schools that enrolled mostly or exclusively children of parents who had immigrated to the United States from Latin American countries, Spanish was an important part of the curriculum since the Spanish spoken by incoming students tended to lack proper grammatical structure. Computer literacy is a growing area of attention for Nativity schools as well, and most of the schools in this study had fairly well-equipped computer labs that were connected to the Internet and received considerable use for student research projects. Knowing that many high-performing high schools expect incoming students to possess a certain level of computer literacy, many Nativity schools sought to strengthen this aspect of their programs.

SUMMER PROGRAMS

Friendships, cooperation, life lessons, leadership, and accepting challenge are some of the themes that are developed during Nativity summer camps. Summer programs serve academic, social, and spiritual purposes and all Nativity schools seek to address these purposes during their summer program regardless of length and location. The summer program at Nativity Mission Center, which began before the school was actually formed, takes place over a seven-week period at Camp Monserrate near Lake Placid, New York, and is supported in large measure by the Julian Reiss Foundation. (This foundation also supports the three-week camp experience for the students at the Nativity school for girls in New York.)

Just as with the advisory groups that are a part of most Nativity schools, the camp experience is designed to bring students together in mixed-age groups for discussions, activities, and living. At the camp for Nativity Mission Center boys, for example, students are housed in mixed-grade cabins of approximately ten students each to facilitate relationships across the grades that help ease the transition for the new students and provide leadership opportunities for the rising eighth graders. Academics occupy some of the morning hours at most of the camps where language arts and mathematics take center stage and children are expected to continue to develop as skilled readers and critical thinkers. Education is also taken out of the classroom on nature hikes and in drama productions. On a July day, I traveled to an off-campus site to observe and talk with rising seventh graders at St. Ignatius Loyola Academy who were conducting an environmental science stream study as part of their summer camp. The St. Ignatius camp experience focuses on academic enrichment at the school for two weeks, followed by two weeks of off-campus research projects, including the stream study, and sports.

Camps have served as an important socialization tool as well. At Camp Monserrate, the staff helps Nativity Mission Center students learn the responsibilities of living in community that include how to treat one another with kindness and respect, how to resolve interpersonal conflicts peacefully, and how to look out for and support one another. According to an alumnus-teacher, the students come to internalize a strong sense of brotherhood at the camp that manifests itself in mutual support, respect, and caring for one another. Boys and girls alike have described their camp experiences as ones that helped to establish a sense of family among the students and teachers at their schools. Teachers who worked at the camps also reported that the camps help the students develop a strong sense of community and internalize the standards for conduct expected at the school, greatly reducing the potential for behavior problems during the academic year.

Leadership development is a very important focus of the camp experiences as well. For example, at the camp for the boys at the Nativity Jesuit Middle School in Milwaukee, which is held at a facility owned by the Jesuit province, a *Camper of the Week* award is given to an eighth grader who demonstrates exceptional leadership. Encouraged and supported by the staff, rising eighth graders are expected to assume leadership roles in their small groups.

The sleepaway summer camps, which include regular prayer services and opportunities for discussions and self-reflection, also provide an excellent context for students' spiritual development. For example, a chapel on the grounds at Camp Monserrate provides a setting for Mass and prayer, and nightly prayer and reflection in the cabins encourage the campers to explore their spiritual beliefs and the implications of these beliefs for right behavior.

I found a fair amount of variation in the nature of the summer programs during my school visits. One Nativity school included in this study operates one camp experience at the school for the incoming fifth-grade students and requires that the girls in the sixth, seventh, and eighth grades attend an approved two-week sleepover camp for which the students apply for scholarship aid with the assistance of the school. The vice principal indicated that a primary objective for this kind of experience is to help the girls develop greater independence and to become acquainted with students from the kind of socioeconomic backgrounds that they will encounter in the private and parochial high schools they will attend. Although this type of camp experience differs considerably from that of other Nativity schools where the students attend camp together, there seems to be no loss of a sense of a caring community among the students.

Not all schools are able to afford an off-campus summer experience for their students. For example, at Mother Seton Academy in Baltimore, students attend morning classes at the school during the summer and take part in recreational and cultural field trips during the two-week camp that contribute to the students' development of social and cultural skills and a sense of belongingness to the school. They also are expected to complete packets of academic material on their own during the summer.

Summer camp experiences are used by many of the Nativity schools as the final screening of candidates for admission to the school. At Mother Seton Academy, for example, I observed a group of approximately fifty girls and boys in large group settings and small classes who were attending a two-week program designed to evaluate how each child would interact and cooperate with teachers and other children and how well each one persisted in the face of academic challenge. Other schools evaluated students' social adjustment at summer sleepaway camps or school-based programs as a final selection tool. At St. Ignatius in Baltimore, for example, as many as forty-five boys who passed through the spring Saturday morning tutoring program that served as an initial screening attend a four-week half-day academic and activity program at the school. From this group, twenty-six boys will be offered admission to the school for the fall. The school year then begins with a three-day retreat off-campus for all seventy to seventy-two students that involves building a sense of community before the start of regular classes.

DIVERSITY CHALLENGES

Most administrators and teachers at the Nativity schools are Caucasian, a factor that would seem to make it difficult for the schools to provide an environment that is culturally responsive to the needs of their students. At the time of the study, ten of eleven presidents or executive directors and six principals or school heads were Caucasian. In addition, 75 percent of Nativity teachers in this study self-identified as Caucasian, 18 percent as black or African American, and only 2.4 percent as Hispanic or Latino. On the other hand, 60 percent of Nativity students self-identified as black or African American, 25 percent as Hispanic or Latino, and nearly 11 percent as biracial, Asian, or "other." Only 4 percent of Nativity school students identified themselves as white or Caucasian.

Despite these differences in racial backgrounds, most students viewed their teachers in a very positive light, consistently indicating that they felt comfortable talking to their teachers and perceived their teachers as caring. In a focus group of parents of Mexican heritage in Milwaukee, the praise for the president and director of graduate support, both middle-aged Caucasian men, was extremely strong and the expression of gratitude for all that these men had done for their children heartfelt. Most parents and students feel that their needs are being met well in the schools. In addition, administrators have helped to establish a strong tradition of parent involvement that has fostered a strong sense of community among parents, students, and school personnel at most of the Nativity schools.

Administrators in all of the schools indicated the struggles they have faced in hiring teachers from racial groups consistent with those of their students and discussed strategies used to recruit teachers of color through job fairs, advertising, involving trustees who are members of minority groups, and direct contact of potential teachers through various Web sites. Two of the nine schools that have been in operation long enough to have alumni who are college graduates have hired alumni as teachers. In fact, at the time of my visit, Nativity Mission Center had three alumni employed at the school, two as faculty and one as graduate support program director. These men felt a particularly strong identification with the mission of the school and a sense of gratitude for what the school gave them that they wanted to convey to the current students.

PARENT INVOLVEMENT

All schools attempt to get their parents involved in the life of the school. At a minimum, parents must come to the school three times a year to pick up their child's report card and discuss his or her academic progress and social development. Most schools go a step further to require parent participation through work projects at the school, helping to prepare food for special celebrations, or providing office assistance. At the Boston boys' school, parents are required to work at the school on Saturdays during the week when their sons' advisory group is assigned daily school cleaning duties. Results of this study showed particularly high levels of participation and engagement in the life of the school among Latino parents and in other schools that actively pursued the involvement of the parents. Parent participation in the life of the school was higher, it seemed, where the students lived in the same community near the school. In schools that admitted children from various parts of the city, parents were not as involved, due in part to the distance between home and school. Job demands on some parents and guardians also contributed to the challenges of parent participation. In most Nativity schools, at least one staff member was instrumental in reaching out to parents in support of the students.

BEYOND THE MODEL

Although all Nativity schools follow the same basic model, a few have sought to incorporate even more into the already extensive school program. Athletic or physical education programs are difficult for many schools to provide because of space limitations in high-density urban areas. Most schools lack outdoor and indoor recreational space and, where open space exists near the schools, the areas present significant safety concerns. However, most Nativity schools have managed to incorporate sports or recreation, or both, as a part of their programs; some even field teams that compete against other schools in sports such as soccer and basketball. St. Ignatius Loyola Academy in Baltimore also includes lacrosse and wrestling among its offerings to the students, and students must board busses for a ten-minute ride to a city park to participate in soccer in the fall and lacrosse in the spring. Other schools have established connections in the community where students can learn to play sports such as tennis and golf.

In the fall of 2005, the Washington Middle School for Girls expanded and moved its sixth, seventh, and eighth grades to a new complex while it added a fourth-grade class to its existing campus. This complex houses several other programs as well, including a boys and girls club, Covenant House of Washington, schools of music and art, and the Washington School of Psychiatry, all of which lend some support to the school. The facility, known as

THEARC (Town Hall Education, Arts, & Recreation Campus, 2006), provides a comprehensive education and health program for underserved children and their families in the Anacostia area of the District of Columbia, in addition to access to a theater, gymnasium, and playground for the school students. This partnership allows the students and the school access to a unique set of opportunities and services.

Also unique among Nativity schools is Epiphany School in Boston that describes itself as providing a "full-service program" (Epiphany, n.d.). Not only does the school admit four children into its fifth grade class each year who live in foster homes, it also selects its students by lottery from among those applicants who qualify financially, giving preferential admission only to siblings of previously enrolled students (as long as their parents or guardians continue to meet the income guidelines). The services funded by the school include medical, optical, dental, psychological, and social services for students whose families are not able to provide for them. The school's outreach team also helps parents access needed social services.

Epiphany and the other Nativity schools that educate both boys and girls separate the boys and girls for academic instruction, and offer opportunities for them to interact together for meals, recess, and afternoon and evening study. This co-institutional arrangement was viewed as a particular strength of the model by graduates (although not preferred by as many current students) because it enabled them to focus on academic learning without the distraction of diverting attention to members of the other sex.

ADVANTAGES OVER COMPARISON SCHOOLS

The Nativity schools have several advantages over the comparison parochial schools included in this study, beginning with the administrative structure. The comparison schools, as with most other parochial schools in Baltimore, have a principal but no president or executive director, development personnel, or graduate support program director. The addition of the administrators who represent the school to the greater city community and direct fund-raising activities enables the Nativity schools to provide a high-quality education without the tuitions that archdiocesan parochial schools must charge. Responsibility for seeking grant funding and lobbying the archdiocese for funds to support its programs falls largely on principals in the comparison parochial schools.

Comparison schools also do not employ any volunteer teachers in their middle school programs and hire only experienced teachers for classroom instruction. Class sizes are larger in the comparison schools and after-school programs are available, but optional. The comparison parochial schools do not have summer programs to help guard against the "summer slide" of students' academic abilities.

Regardless of the variations in the ways the Nativity schools in this study applied the original model, certain features were evident throughout all the schools. These features included the small school and class size, the low student–teacher ratios, and the extended day for tutoring and homework assistance that provided more engaged learning time than other parochial or public middle schools could. In addition, all Nativity schools offer a summer program that included academic enhancement and activities to support social and spiritual development, as well as a graduate support program to help their students succeed in high school and beyond. Personnel in all of the schools understood their mission to educate "men and women for others" in the tradition of the Society of Jesus and were exceptionally dedicated educators, regardless of their level of experience. The only way in which I could say that a small minority of schools deviated significantly from the original model was in the limited use of volunteer teachers. In addition, the specialness of the Nativity schools with the programs described that included adult education or a "full-service" program provide food for thought for other Nativity schools and individuals and groups considering the possibility of joining their ranks. I'll return to this and other issues in the final chapter.

FOUR

Academic Success

IN THIS CHAPTER I examine just how successful Nativity schools are in advancing the academic competencies of their students and address factors that contribute to the levels of success experienced by the students. In examining this issue, I present statistics on standardized test scores in reading and mathematics, high school attendance and graduation rates, college entrance rates, and quantitative and qualitative analyses of factors that are related to academic performance measures. Findings show that students in most, but not all, Nativity schools experience remarkable academic gains, and factors such as small classes, a high level of academic challenge, an extended school day, and supportive and caring teachers and administrators contribute to this student academic success.

ANALYSIS OF STANDARDIZED TEST SCORES

In today's educational climate that emphasizes assessment and adequate yearly progress (AYP), no evaluation of school success can be conducted without an examination of student performance and performance gains on standardized achievement tests. Although the particular test administered in each Nativity school varies, all the schools administer standardized tests in reading and mathematics achievement at least once each year, with the first test usually in the fall or spring of the first year of attendance. The results are impressive.

Table 4.1 summarizes test score data for the seven Nativity schools and the two comparison parochial schools that educate children who have backgrounds and experience living situations very similar to those of Nativity students. (These data for each of the Nativity and comparison schools can be found in Appendix C.)

Because of the nature of scoring of standardized tests and the difficulty in calculating the actual amount of gain exhibited by each student, I established

TABLE 4.1
Standardized Test Scores and Attendance Data for Members of the Class of 2004

School	7th Grade Math (% ≥ GL)[1]	Math: % of Students Improving ≥ 1 GE/yr[2]	7th Grade Reading (% ≥ GL)[1]	Reading: % of Students Improving ≥ 1 GE/yr[2]	7th Grade GPA	Attendance Rate
Seven Nativity Schools (N = 199)	57.1%	69.7%	61.4%	76.9%	83.5	96.8%
Comparison Schools (N = 118)	23.2%	40.7%	28.4%	50.8%	80.7	96.9%
Chi-Square Tests	38.24*	25.71*	34.68*	22.78*		

Notes: [1]Percentage of students scoring at or above grade level (GL) at the time of test administration. [2]Percent of students showing grade equivalent (GE) gains in standardized test scores equal to or greater than the number of years they attended the school. *$p \leq .001$.

that a student was performing at or above grade level if he or she scored at the 48th percentile or higher on the test. For those schools that reported scores as grade equivalents (GEs), a student was considered at or above grade level if her or his GE was at least as high as the level corresponding to the student's grade level and school month at the time of the test administration (e.g., a GE of 7.1 for a seventh grader tested in October). I then computed the percentage of students who tested at or above grade level in seventh grade at each school. In addition, to examine gains in test scores, I computed whether or not a student gained one GE or more per year during the years that the student attended the school. (For scores provided to us as percentiles, a gain of one GE or more was indicated by an increase of one percentile point or more per year of attendance.) This approach to gains in student standardized test score performance has been used in previous research to assess achievement gains (see Balfanz & Byrnes, 2006).

These results showed that 57.1 percent of Nativity students were performing at or above grade level in math and 61.4 percent at or above grade level in reading in the seventh grade. This compares to 23.2 percent and 28.4 percent in math and reading, respectively, for comparison school students.

With respect to gains in standardized test scores, the percentage of Nativity students who improved at least one GE per year of attendance in math was 57.1 percent and 76.9 percent in reading. For the comparison schools, 40.7 percent of students improved one or more GEs per year in math and 50.8 percent did so in reading. As shown in Table 4.1, all statistical comparisons between Nativity and comparison schools that examined seventh-grade achievement levels and gains were statistically significant. At the same time, the variation in standardized test score performance among Nativity schools, with some at levels similar to those of the comparison schools, suggests the need to examine differences among the schools' programs, an issue addressed later in this chapter.

Data summarizing student standardized test score performance at urban public middle schools showed that public school students lagged far behind the Nativity school and comparison school students. For example, for a sample of 740 seventh-grade students in six middle schools in Baltimore, where a large percentage of Nativity students would be assigned had they not attended a private or parochial middle school, the mean national Terra Nova percentile scores in math and reading were 27.2 and 29.2, respectively, for the 2002–2003 academic year. These figures suggest that the percentages of these public school students who were achieving at or above grade level in reading and math were lower than those of students at the comparison schools where the mean percentile scores were 34.6 in math and 34.9 in reading. With the majority of Nativity school students testing at or above grade level in math and reading, the mean percentile scores for them would be greater than 50 for both tests. When making these comparisons, it would be important to recognize that, in the six comparison public urban middle schools, the percentage of students qualifying for the federal full and reduced meal program ranged from 66 to 94 percent. In the comparison parochial schools, 90 percent of students qualified; in the Nativity schools, 94 percent were eligible.

By any measure, middle school students attending urban public schools are performing poorly on national assessments. For example, the 2003 NAEP urban assessments of eighth graders in mathematics and reading show that in large central city districts only 21 percent of students are performing at a level considered *proficient* or above in mathematics (National Center for Educational Statistics, NCES, 2004a, 2004b). In reading, the percentage of eighth graders performing at this level is 20 percent. In Boston and New York, cities where five of the Nativity schools in the present study are located, the percentages of students performing at this level were 12 and 21 percent, respectively, in math and 16 and 22 percent, respectively, in reading. Although these data do not translate into statistics that can be used to compare with students' standardized test scores on Terra Nova or Iowa tests, they clearly indicate that urban children attending public schools are performing poorly—and at a much lower level than students in the Nativity schools.

FURTHER EDUCATIONAL
ATTAINMENT AND ACHIEVEMENT

Additional data collected from eight of the Nativity schools or provided by the Nativity Educational Centers Network show the level of success students demonstrate in the years following their graduation. For the class of 2004, with 160 original members, 140, or 87.5 percent, having graduated with their class, four remained in the school, seven had been dismissed for behavioral problems, and nine left the school voluntarily. Of the 140 graduates, 113 (81 percent) were attending Catholic or other private high schools and 26 (19 percent) were enrolled at regional, magnet, vocational, or charter public high schools, with one graduate unaccounted for. Six of these Nativity schools graduated ninety-nine students in 2000, with eighty-six (86.9 percent) graduating from high school in four years and only two dropping out prior to graduation without obtaining a GED. Of the seventy-nine high school graduates the schools were able to further identify, sixty-two (78.5 percent) attended a four-year college, eleven (13.9 percent) attended a two-year college, five (6.3 percent) were working, and one had joined the military.

Results similar to these have been reported consistently for Nativity schools. For example, the Web site for the network of Nativity and San Miguel schools boasts a four-year high school graduation rate of nearly 90 percent (NativityMiguel Network of Schools, n.d.). In addition, Podsiadlo and Philliber (2003) reported that 81 percent of the students who graduated from Nativity Mission Center between 1989 and 1996 completed high school. They compared this result to a graduation rate of 66 percent for Latino students who entered New York City public schools in 1997. For further comparison, the Education Week online Research Center (Editorial Projects in Education, 2007) reported that the graduation rate for black and Hispanic students in New York State was 42 percent and 36 percent, respectively, and 59 percent and 46 percent, respectively, in Massachusetts, in 2002.

These data show that the Nativity schools are indeed fulfilling their goal of preparing students for academic success and the pursuit of higher education. At the same time, the school administrators were quick to acknowledge that they did not view college attendance and graduation as the sole indicator of success for their students. The schools also take pride in their graduates who have successful careers in the military or take on the challenge of regular employment after high school or demonstrate leadership, competence, and right living in other ways.

FACTORS CONTRIBUTING TO ACADEMIC SUCCESS

The Nativity school model incorporates several components that have been shown in research studies on effective middle school education to contribute to student achievement. These characteristics and practices were studied in an attempt to determine which seem to be most influential in the success of Nativity school students. To this end, in this section, characteristics of high- and low-performing Nativity schools, comparison parochial schools included in this study, and other schools from the research literature are examined and compared. These characteristics and practices include school size, size of student groups for instruction, length of the school day and year, time students spend in instruction, study, and remediation beyond the normal school day, characteristics of the learning environment in the schools, levels of student engagement in learning, admissions practices, qualifications of the teachers, involvement levels of parents, administrator characteristics, and characteristics of student attitudes and perceptions of the school environment.

SCHOOL AND CLASS SIZE

First, with respect to characteristics of the schools themselves, few schools enroll a student body as small as Nativity schools do. (One public urban PreK–8 school in Baltimore for which test score data were previously included enrolled only thirty-two students in grades six through eight.[1]) Restricted in part by the small size of the buildings procured for operating the schools, Nativity schools enroll between fifty-two and ninety-six students. In contrast, the comparison schools included in the present study enrolled seventy-five and 130 sixth-, seventh-, and eighth-grade students, respectively, in the middle school components of their larger PreK–8 schools. In addition, urban public middle schools are rarely as small as the Nativity schools or other parochial schools.

But the size of the student body of a school is not likely to be the only factor that explains student achievement success. Nativity school administrators indicate that they realize that, if they had the space, they could educate more children and accomplish a similar level of academic success. The small size is valuable as well as important in meeting their goals of the development of the students' leadership skills and their social, spiritual, and emotional lives. Also, the variation in levels of student academic performance among Nativity schools suggests that we examine factors other than school size.

With respect to size of groups of students for instruction, as well as student–teacher ratios, Nativity schools demonstrate an advantage over the comparison parochial schools included in this study as well as most urban public middle schools. My observations show that these schools take great care to be informed about the learning challenges of each of their students and provide one-on-one and small group instruction to children with the

---

1. Mean seventh-grade reading and math percentile test scores were 34 and 27, respectively, and 66 percent of its students qualified for the federal free and reduced meal program.

greatest academic challenges and skill deficits. The Nativity schools typically divide up the students at a particular grade level into two (and sometimes more) ability groups, with the students who struggle the most placed in the smaller groups. In no case did I observe more than sixteen students in a classroom for instruction, a practice substantiated by teachers and principals I interviewed. Because Nativity schools hire several volunteer or intern teachers (young adults with bachelor degrees from highly regarded colleges and universities but little or no teaching experience), they are able to provide the kind of small group instruction that larger parochial and public schools cannot afford. In addition, a small but growing number of the schools also employ a reading specialist who can pull struggling readers out of class for individualized instruction.

INSTRUCTIONAL TIME

The amount of time during which students are receiving instruction and tutoring in quiet and focused classrooms is significantly greater in Nativity schools than in other middle schools, private or public. Not only is the amount of class time greater in Nativity schools, the smaller instructional groups ensure that students remain engaged in learning. This *engaged learning time*, time during which students are truly involved in learning activities, is certainly one factor that sets Nativity schools apart from other schools. Schools offer high levels of learning time by providing small class sizes for instruction, individual attention from teachers, tutoring for those students who need additional assistance, required evening study, and weekend study sessions for students who are not keeping up with the academic demands of the school. Nativity schools engage their students in more learning time than I have observed in any other middle school program. Even in elite independent schools, such as the one in which I taught a number of years ago, where class sizes are small and students are very engaged academically, students are engaged for fewer total hours during the day. As I discuss next, my school visits indicate to me that engaged learning time, in particular that time devoted to the development of math and reading skills, is a major factor that helps explain the outstanding levels of student achievement and achievement gains in the Nativity schools.

Of course, in addition to simply being engaged in learning activities, students need to be engaged in those that are beneficial—tasks that enable students to extend their learning into the upper region of their zone of proximal development—that is, a level of understanding, as identified by Vygotsky, that students are not able to reach on their own but require the assistance of a more knowledgeable person. This type of mentoring or instruction would need to come from a teacher or tutor who knows how to scaffold a child's learning from his or her initial level of understanding and who has a curriculum available to help a child achieve a higher level of understanding. I will discuss the issue of teacher qualifications in Nativity schools more in chapter 6, but wish to point out here that the quality of the curriculum (the *what*) and instruction (the *how*) are crucial factors in helping students understand material and develop academic skills at a higher level. As I discussed in chapter 3, curriculums at the Nativity schools are fairly strong and rigorous.

School and Classroom Climate

Small school and class size, and a philosophy reflected in the Jesuit notion of *cura personalis* (care of the whole person), make it possible for schools to provide a climate for learning that is supportive, respectful, and caring, factors that contribute significantly to student engagement in learning (National Middle School Association, 2003; Trimble, 2004). As both quantitative and qualitative data from this study show, school and classroom climate factors clearly played a role in the academic success of Nativity students.

I first examined student survey data to identify climate factors that distinguished Nativity schools from the comparison parochial schools. These comparisons (see Appendix D) show that Nativity school students, when compared to the comparison school students, viewed the peer social climate of their schools as more supportive of developing friendships and the overall school climate as more enjoyable with rules more fair, although comparison school students perceived their principal as more caring and supportive. Nativity students also rated their math and language arts class environments as more conducive to learning with teachers who were supportive and caring. There were no significant differences in student perceptions of their self-esteem, intrinsic motivation for learning, or difficulties adjusting to school. These findings, along with results of correlation analyses relating climate variables to student academic performance, suggest that the perceptions of the school and classroom climate that favored Nativity schools are ones that affect student academic achievement (see also Fenzel, Domingues, & Raughley, 2006; Fenzel & Monteith, 2008). A recent analysis involving African American students from the Nativity study (Fenzel & O'Brennan, 2007) showed that, when students perceive their school climate as enjoyable with rules that are fair, they are engaged more in learning and perform better in the classroom.

Findings from interviews with students and their responses to open-ended items on the written surveys support the effect that the friendly and supportive, yet academically challenging, environment of Nativity schools has on student academic engagement and performance. Students in focus group interviews uniformly reported that teachers, although strict, were highly respectful and caring. Many students noted that they treasured the amount of time that teachers were willing to sit with them to help them with their work and listen to their concerns. Students reported a highly consistent pattern of challenge and support from their teachers and administrators, characteristics of school environments that provide a good fit with young adolescents' developmental needs and support their academic development and success (Eccles, Wigfield, Midgley, Reuman, MacIver, & Feldlaufer, 1993; Fenzel, Magaletta, & Peyrot, 1997).

Summer Camps and Programs

Mandatory summer programs, a feature of Nativity schools that distinguishes them from many other schools for urban children placed at risk, also engage students in academic learning that contributes to their academic skill development and achievement levels. School-level analyses using the Spearman rank-order test showed fairly strong relations between the number of summer program days for a Nativity school and a school's percentage of students achieving at or above grade level in math ($r_s = .61$) and reading ($r_s = .86$). Similar correlations were found for the relation of summer program days to the percentage of students showing gains of one or more grade levels per year in math achievement ($r_s = .65$) and reading achievement ($r_s = .62$). In all the Nativity schools, approximately two to three hours each day during the summer program are devoted specifically to academic learning and skill development, with additional time set aside for independent reading.

Admissions Policies and Practices

Since most Nativity schools do not select students at random, I examined the manner in which these schools admit students as a possible contributor to students' academic success. Most schools use some criteria to select students for the limited number of seats available, with all schools beginning their evaluation process in the spring or summer prior to the students' matriculation. Interviews with school personnel showed me that, in general, the longer a school has been in operation, the greater its pool of applicants and the more the school personnel have learned about the kinds of characteristics of the children and their families that increase the likelihood of student success. Several administrators reported that, in the early years of the school, school officials tended to select those children who demonstrated the greatest need (however that was defined), but realized that some of the students were not able to succeed in the demanding educational programs. These students tended to be those with very difficult living situations or severe learning difficulties.

Two factors that most schools have come to recognize as important for school success in their programs are that students demonstrate a desire to work hard to succeed and behavior that is cooperative and respectful. Most of the schools do not select students with special needs that they lack the staff to support. One school reported that it does not admit potentially strong students if they have been accepted to another middle school program of good quality in order to open up a space for a child without such an option. Although most schools attempt to identify students who possess the potential to succeed in their demanding academic programs, doing so is not always easy. Clearly the schools are not selecting students with outstanding academic credentials, nor are they selecting students with severe academic deficits. Epiphany school in Boston stands out as an example of a school in which students succeed at high levels without attempts to screen its applicants; except for siblings of current students, it selects students by lottery from the pool of applicants who meet income requirements, with 20 percent from the foster-care system. Because this approach brings several children to the school with significant learning, emotional, and behavioral challenges, the school has committed resources to provide or secure the professional support they require.

FAMILY CHARACTERISTICS

Characteristics of the children's home lives are also factors that experienced Nativity school administrators have acknowledged as important influences on the levels of student academic success. Across the board, the schools that are able to be more selective admit students from families where there are sufficient indicators of adequate family support for learning. At least one Nativity school conducts interviews in the applicants' homes to examine the kind of environment in which students live and to assess the extent to which they view the parents as committed to and capable of supporting their child with the demands of a Nativity education. Results presented elsewhere (Fenzel, 2003; Fenzel et al., 2006) have shown high levels of parental involvement in most Nativity schools and a relationship between levels of parental involvement in the school and students' report card grades. Also, results from the present study demonstrated that students who perceived their parents as more supportive indicated higher levels of intrinsic motivation and were more likely to post gains in standardized test performance.

COMPARISON OF TWO NATIVITY SCHOOLS

Recognizing, however, that some variation does exist among Nativity schools with respect to student academic performance, I conducted additional analyses to shed some light on the factors that distinguish a higher performing from a lower performing school. I identified two schools for girls for this analysis by virtue of the mean performance of their students in the class of 2004 for whom test score data from their fifth, sixth, and seventh grades were available. As shown in Table 4.2, the two schools had very different profiles of student achievement on standardized tests in reading and math, with students

TABLE 4.2
Percentages of Students at Two Nativity Schools
Performing at or above Grade Level

Reading Test Performance	5th Grade	6th Grade*	7th Grade*
School A	41%	71%	79%
School B	31%	35%	38%
Mathematics Test Performance	5th Grade	6th Grade	7th Grade*
School A	44%	58%	86%
School B	23%	33%	44%

Note: *Chi-square tests significant at $p \leq .05$ or better.

in School A demonstrating a greater degree of growth in both math and reading achievement over the two years. Students in School B were performing at lower levels, on average, upon entry into the school when compared to School A students. Although these differences were not statistically significant, they hint at a lower level of academic preparedness that may make it more difficult for students to realize substantial gains.

Table 4.3 shows the results of a series of t-test analyses comparing a number of the factors previously examined for these two schools. Results were quite striking in that students in School A held significantly more positive perceptions of two climate factors—the learning climate of their math and language arts classes and the peer social climate of the school. In addition, these students perceived themselves as having less difficulty adjusting to the demands of the school. Also, teachers at the higher performing school viewed their students as more engaged academically and assigned significantly higher report card grades. On the other hand, differences in the students' perceptions of their school as enjoyable and the rules fair and their levels of intrinsic motivation did not reach statistical significance.

During my visits, I saw programs in both schools that provided the students with a caring environment that encouraged them to set and meet high academic standards. In focus group interviews with seventh and eighth graders at both schools, the students reported that the teachers were strict but also caring. Both schools had experienced instructional leaders who demonstrated high levels of caring and challenged the girls to excel. In both schools, teachers worked long hours and participated in regular faculty meetings to address curriculum, instructional planning, and classroom management issues. Also, both schools offered arts enrichment activities for the students and employed reading specialists to work with children with the greatest needs in reading.

TABLE 4.3

T-Test Comparison of Student and Teacher Perceptions and Student GPA
of a High-Performing and Lower Performing Nativity School

Student Perceptions	High-Performing School (N = 51)	Lower Performing School (N = 47)	t	Cohen's d
Math and LA Class Climate	3.35 (.34)	3.09 (.36)	3.71***	.75
Peer Social Climate	3.51 (.42)	3.18 (.50)	3.62***	.73
School Enjoyable and Fair	3.20 (.51)	3.10 (.58)	.91	.18
School Adjustment Difficulty	2.42 (1.37)	3.25 (1.19)	−3.19**	.64
Intrinsic Motivation	3.13 (.52)	2.98 (.46)	1.49	.30
Teacher Perception of Student Engagement	2.04 (.32)	1.76 (.36)	3.20**	.65
Grade Point Average	88.4 (4.7; N = 31)	76.3 (9.7; N = 29)	6.09***	1.61

Two-tailed values: $*p \leq .05$, $**p \leq .01$, $***p \leq .001$.

With respect to structural features, both schools educate girls in grades five through eight, although certain features of School A may have enabled it to provide an environment that was more conducive to student learning. This school has well-designed classrooms, including a science lab equipped with lab materials, whereas School B has few enclosed classroom spaces and lacks materials needed for much hands-on science work. Math class in School B, which met only for four periods each week, was held in a semi-open space adjacent to the breakfast and lunch area that contributed to student distractions. The student–teacher ratio in School A was somewhat more favorable, due in part to the larger number of volunteer teachers on staff. In addition to the different ethnic and cultural backgrounds of the students in the two schools, School A had been in operation for a few years longer, providing its administration with more time to make adjustments to the school program and attract students with a greater potential to succeed. The age of the school also has implications for the state of the curriculum, with School B administrators recognizing the need for further curriculum development.

Some clear differences emerged with respect to the school climate as well. Girls at the higher performing school were more likely to report that teachers made learning fun and to reflect a sense of community among the students. By seventh and eighth grade, the girls at this school felt confident and capable and possessed a strong sense of belongingness to the school community to a somewhat greater degree than did girls at School B. Findings from my interviews and observations suggested, too, that the students in School B brought more family difficulties and more behavioral and emotional challenges with them than did students at School A. I surmised that the headmistress of School B also had a more difficult time getting the parents involved in the school and their children's education. I also saw signs that the issues that were likely to be affecting student achievement were in the process of being addressed. In fact, School B was preparing to move to a facility that would include better classroom space.

Taken together, the survey data and the observational and interview data from my school visits showed how important the social and academic climate is to student engagement and academic success, and the extent to which family difficulties and students' emotional challenges can undermine student academic performance. Nativity schools that are more successful do a wonderful job of creating a sense of community where respect and caring abound and where students are challenged academically and classrooms are run well with effective instruction. In addition, the academic challenge is complemented with adequate support through homework help, tutoring, and remediation in the extended day programs. The more successful schools also receive a high level of cooperation and support from parents, a factor that is enhanced by admissions practices that place a high level of importance on parental buy-in. (See also Fenzel & Monteith, 2008.)

GRADUATE SUPPORT

An important contributor to student academic success and attainment after graduation from Nativity schools is the graduate support program. Through this program, all Nativity schools provide valuable services to their students throughout their high school years. Beginning in the eighth-grade year, the graduate support program (GSP) director arranges for classes to prepare eighth graders for private school admissions tests and assists the families with the application process. This person also monitors the academic progress of the graduates, accompanies the graduates on college visits, arranges for SAT preparation classes, and assists families with the college application process. GSP directors also arrange for tutoring help for their graduates in high school when needed, schedule events to bring graduates back to the school and in contact with one another, and even counsel the graduates who face significant stressors in high school. Also, in order to best serve the graduates, the GSP director teaches at least one class to the Nativity students so that the director and the students can begin to know one another before they leave the school.

The GSP director at the Nativity Mission School is an alumnus of the school who grew up in the same neighborhood as many of the students. He graduated from a parochial high school and a private four-year college and took the director position soon after college graduation. His family background and alumnus status enable him to relate well with the students and their families. He works most days from 1 until 8 P.M., holding study sessions Monday through Thursday for boys in each of the four high school classes and supervising a Friday evening recreation program. In addition, he monitors graduates' high school adjustment and progress, teaches weekly SAT preparation classes for the high school seniors, follows up with families of boys who do not come to evening study when expected or who are not doing well in high school, and conducts workshops for parents and guardians on high school and college admissions. He also sponsors two alumni events each year and participates in efforts to encourage successful alumni to interact with current Nativity students and help support the school financially.

In virtually all of the Nativity schools, the graduate support program directors work hard to maintain contact with their graduates who are college students, encouraging them to persist to graduation even when they are stressed by social and family problems. Counseling ends up being a significant part of the job, involving graduates themselves and sometimes even the families as well, who may find it difficult to imagine their sons leaving home to attend college.

SUMMARY

That students who attend Nativity schools improve their academic skills and perform at outstanding levels as a result of the Nativity education is indisputable. However, the variation in the levels and rates of student academic development suggests that some factors contribute to academic success more than others. While small school and class size and characteristics of the students and their families certainly play a role, these features tell only part of the story of student success. Results presented in this chapter suggest that, in addition to a strong curriculum delivered by skilled and committed instructors, factors contributing substantially to student academic progress are related to the climate of learning, mutual respect, and community that is built into the fabric of the school. Results indicate that students who feel cared for and respected and are held to consistently high standards usually succeed and excel. As research has shown, the setting of high expectations must be accompanied by structures and processes that support students as they struggle to meet these expectations. Nativity schools provide such support in the form of afternoon and evening study sessions and tutoring. Summer programs that have a substantial academic component also contribute to student success by reinforcing and advancing student competencies during a time when too many children disengage from academic learning. Given the fact that most students enter Nativity schools one or two years below grade level and with some from low-performing public elementary schools, the high levels of academic and emotional support that the schools provide in a structure that engages the students in learning for more hours than other schools account for the high levels of academic success and educational attainment of Nativity students.

FIVE

Social, Emotional, Spiritual, and Physical Development

AFTER CONSUMING a breakfast of peanut butter on graham crackers plus juice, the group of approximately fifty girls shuffles over to a corner of the cafeteria where several rows of folding chairs await their arrival. Dressed in uniform blouses, slacks, and distinctive African cloth vests, the students of the Washington Middle School for Girls take their seats facing a podium where three students stand ready to begin the morning prayer service. The service commences with the singing of *Let Every Voice Sing*, the black National Anthem. The students then take their seats and distribute booklets of prayers to one another after which one of the student leaders reads a reflection for the day and leads the students in reciting prayers. The school president, Sr. Mary, makes a few announcements, acknowledges the girls who participated in a recent Walk for the Homeless, and thanks the students for bringing in food for the upcoming Thanksgiving dinner to be held at the school.

At Nativity Preparatory School in Boston, the boys hustle up the stairs past the principal and gather in their class groups, each named for a figure in Jesuit history, in a large gathering space at the end of the hall. The principal makes a few announcements as the boys stand quietly in lines facing the podium. Then the chaplain, a Jesuit priest, reads a brief Bible passage and suggests a focus for individual reflection. Following this, he invites the students and teachers to offer prayer requests. Numerous requests are offered that include prayers for the success of the school soccer team that afternoon, as well as for an ill grandmother, an uncle who was struggling with drug addiction, and a sibling serving time in jail. The service ends with the students and teachers holding hands in a large circle around the perimeter of the room reciting the Lord's Prayer and St. Ignatius's *Prayer for Generosity,* a plea to God to help the individual learn to be generous and to serve and give of oneself without the expectation of reward.

Routines such as these mark the beginning of the school day at most of the Nativity schools I visited and provide one of several avenues for students' social, emotional, and spiritual development—tasks at which Nativity schools succeed in an impressive manner.

Nativity schools place a high value on the development of their students' spiritual lives. In addition to morning assemblies, the schools offer a number of activities and structures designed to help students live reflective lives committed to caring for others and seeking justice. These values are reflected in the statement on the Nativity Network (n.d.) Web site that declared that network schools promote:

> a respect for the dignity and potential of each person, a responsibility to assist the poor and those in need, a strong sense of community within the one family of God, and the obligation to promote a society characterized by social justice. ("About Nativity Educational Centers Network")

These values are consistent with those espoused in documents that describe the characteristics of a Jesuit education (e.g., Jesuit Secondary Education Association, JSEA, n.d.). For example, the JSEA document affirms that a Jesuit education contributes to the total formation, or development, of each individual, includes a religious dimension that permeates the entire educational program, insists on individual care and concern for each person, encourages a life-long openness to growth, seeks to form "men and women for others," and manifests a particular concern for the materially poor. It is an education that focuses on the formation of the whole human person for a life of service to the world. In schools not affiliated with the Jesuits, similar values are incorporated in school philosophies and programming.

In the Nativity model schools, the goals of a Nativity education and the expectations of the students are made clear from the start. For example, Nativity Mission Center makes these goals and expectations explicit in the Nativity Pledge, which reads:

> I pledge this day, with *INTEGRITY* and *PRIDE*,
> My continued support for the Spirit of Nativity:
> A Spirit of *COMMUNITY* not selfishness;
> A Spirit of *RESPECT* for each person I encounter;
> A Spirit of *DIGNITY* for who I am;
> A Spirit of *RESPONSIBILITY* for who I will become and
> How I will act in *SERVICE* of others in need;
> May this Spirit grow in me today and
> May the Spirit of Nativity forever thrive!
> (Nativity Mission Center, 2003–2004).

At the Washington Middle School for Girls, the students sign the Student Pledge in which each student affirms that she is "a member of a community that prays, works, and plays together." They pledge also to treat themselves, "other students, and adults with dignity and respect" and to "listen to God's voice within . . . and seek to follow that voice wherever it leads."

In this chapter, I describe ways in which Nativity schools succeed in their efforts to graduate responsible students of integrity and pride who are committed to actively caring for and serving others. During my visits, students, teachers, and administrators provided several examples of formal and informal programs that support the development of their students, spiritually, socially, emotionally, and physically in order to prepare them for lives of service. The small size of the Nativity schools enables teachers and administrators to see to these developmental needs of their students, needs that have not been met before in their schools and that may not be met in their homes.

PROGRAMS THAT PROMOTE STUDENT DEVELOPMENT

Social, emotional, spiritual, and physical developmental needs are addressed and met through a number of structures at Nativity schools. In nearly all schools, common elements include a morning prayer and reflection service that opens the school day, religion and social skills classes, small advisory groups, retreats, counseling, school duties, community service projects, sports teams, family programs, and after-school, weekend, and summer camp programs.

RELIGIOUS SERVICES

At all of the schools I visited, except one, the school day opened with a whole-school assembly that included morning prayer or reflection, or both. At most of the schools, a small group of students led the service or activity, announcements were made, and students were invited to offer prayers for people they wanted to remember. At these assemblies, students often are singled out because of special accomplishments. At Academy Prep in St. Petersburg, students assemble on the outdoor basketball court and offer prayers, although the school has no religious affiliation.

Assemblies referred to as *Chapel* take the place of morning prayer at some schools. Although Chapel may take on the format of a religious service, it is also similar to the morning prayer services and provides an opportunity for students to reflect on issues of community, respect, doing one's best, or discovering one's purpose. At the Episcopal school in Boston, I attended the weekly communion service held in the latter part of the morning. Students and alumni often expressed how much they appreciated the opportunities for such reflection and prayer.

At the Jesuit Nativity schools, in particular, Jesuit practices that include what is known as the *Examen* are used to provide a framework for student self-reflection during the school day and in summer programs. The *Examen* process leads students to reflect on three types of questions that address their actions over the previous twenty-four hours: (1) What am I most grateful for? or What do I feel was pleasing to God? (2) What do I regret? or Where did I fall short? and (3) How will I strive to make the next twenty-four hours different? Students, faculty, and staff at Jesuit secondary schools and colleges are familiar with the *Examen*.

At St. Ignaitus Loyola Academy in Baltimore, teachers are instructed in the principles of Jesuit spirituality and education and encouraged to incorporate spiritual activities in their courses. In the classes I observed, one teacher started class with the students offering prayer intentions and reciting the Lord's Prayer in Latin, and in another class students began the period with a recitation of the Ignatian *Prayer for Generosity*. Students also pray before meals and attend Chapel once a week where they are led in reflection activities that address spiritual and personal development themes.

One school had developed a curriculum based on principles of Catholic social teaching that included topics related to human dignity, human rights, solidarity with underserved persons, and caring for creation. Each month a particular principle was addressed during prayer services and assemblies and was often reinforced through a particular community service project in which the students and faculty participated.

CURRICULUM

Religious faith and personal development are important parts of the curriculum that are addressed at all schools. All religiously affiliated schools include religion as a regular part of the academic curriculum and some schools also include courses that address issues related to students' social-emotional development. Religion courses tend to focus on Judeo-Christian content related to the Old and New Testaments but also expose students to the customs and beliefs of other religious traditions. The curriculum at Mother Seton Academy, for example, calls for the study of the Old Testament in sixth grade, the New Testament in seventh grade, and contemporary moral issues in eighth grade. St. Ignatius Loyola Academy follows a similar curriculum in sixth and seventh grades and focuses more on several of the world's religions and issues of social justice in eighth grade. Although most Nativity schools are operated by Catholic religious orders, they are sensitive to the spiritual orientations and needs of the students who are not Catholic, as a majority of Nativity students follow other religious traditions.

An important part of the curriculum at most Nativity schools contains courses that address life issues related to interpersonal conflict, sexuality, drug abuse, and the like. These courses meet once a week and some use a text, such as *Family Alive*, that serves as a springboard for discussion. The president of the Nativity Jesuit Middle School in Milwaukee, a Jesuit priest, taught the course weekly to each of the three classes of boys. In a class of seventeen boys in the eighth grade that I observed, he made use of a vignette about a man who had been abused as a child in a foster home and arrested at age seventeen to address issues of family struggles, foster homes, child abuse, and domestic violence, issues not unfamiliar to a large percentage of Nativity students.

The curriculum for the *Skills and Issues* classes at St. Ignatius Loyola Academy focuses on study skills and adolescent interpersonal and health issues, including sexuality and drug use, in sixth grade, topics that are reinforced and expanded upon in seventh and eighth grade to also address consumerism, gender stereotyping, and social responsibility. The director of the graduate support program teaches the course for the eighth graders and the principal for the seventh graders. This program of courses is designed to help students cope effectively with the personal and family challenges they face and then help extend their self-awareness to an understanding of larger social issues and a commitment to working for social change.

ADVISORIES

Small group advisories in which a teacher meets regularly with a small group or six to eight students provide a forum for students to address concerns that they have and for the teacher-advisors to lead discussions on issues of concern to the staff. Advisories serve as a context for discussing topics such as motivation, drug abuse prevention, respectful attitudes and behaviors, and health and nutrition issues and for commending boys on their accomplishments. They also promote close relationships among the students and between the students and the teacher-advisor. Each advisory group contains students from all grades in the school and some are formed for the year during the summer camp program. One eighth-grade student at St. Ignatius Loyola Academy described the advisory groups as good forums for addressing issues of respect, mature behavior, and courage. Consistent with the literature on effective middle schools that recommends the implementation of such groups, the advisories allow students get to know at least one teacher particularly well and help school personnel identify any difficulties that students may be experiencing. Time is set aside once a week for these groups to meet with their advisor.

CAMPS, AFTER-SCHOOL PROGRAMS, AND EXCURSIONS

Summer camps provide one of the more important contexts for addressing issues of leadership, community building, respecting and taking care of one another, and helping one another succeed, and for developing student autonomy and identity, two important adolescent developmental tasks. By grouping heterogeneously by age, the camps help to build friendships across the grades and enable younger students to feel more a part of the community of students. Also, by having a very small student-to-counselor ratio, the students have many opportunities to get close to adults they will be working with at the school or who are alumni of the school and to receive the support some need to achieve greater self-confidence. At the camps, students learn to trust each other and to resolve interpersonal conflicts in a mature manner.

At the January 2004 national Nativity Network Gathering of teachers and administrators, Mark Lardner, the director of the summer camp at Nativity Mission Center, outlined the three components of their camp: social, spiritual, and academic. He spoke of the various social skills that are addressed in small groups, including using good table manners, showing respect for peers and adults, and learning coping behaviors that differ from those they have learned on the street. The staff helps students learn to make decisions and behave with positive goals in mind, rather than out of fear of punishment, and to trust and depend on each other. With the guidance of their adult leader, the boys then process how well they did with their day in evening small-group reflections.

The spiritual development of the boys is integrated with the social goals of the camp where goals of respect and care for others and being "men for others" are incorporated into nightly prayer and reflection activities and addressed in daily morning prayer services and Sunday Mass. To help the students keep the focus on the social, spiritual, and academic goals of the camp, no radio, television, or other expressions of popular culture are permitted. The camp is considered the beginning of the school year and includes the boys most recently admitted to the school.

The camp programs at other Nativity schools incorporate daily prayer and reflection as well. For example, at Nativity Jesuit School in Milwaukee, boys are led in the Ignatian practice of the *Examen* that focuses on a review of their daily successes and failures and the keeping of a journal of their self-reflections. The students continue the practice of the *Examen* when they return to their regular school regimen.

St. Ignatius Loyola Academy, also a Jesuit school, includes many of the same elements in the sleepaway portion of its summer camp program during two weeks in June for rising seventh and eighth graders. There are a host of sports and other kinds of activities in which the boys participate daily after an hour of morning academic sessions. These activities enable the students to practice social skills of teamwork and respect and the eighth graders to emerge as school leaders. This camp holds a campfire at night for a reflection that is led by one of the staff or one of the eighth graders, and the older students prepare and act out a respectful drama production that pokes fun at the teachers. In addition, the beginning of the school year is marked by a three-day retreat at this same campsite for all students, who spend some of the time meeting in their new advisory groups; it helps the students focus on the behaviors and attitudes expected of them during the school year and begin the process of mutual care and support among all school members. This marks the first opportunity for the students in all three grades to come together, get to know one another, and develop cross-grade friendships.

Some schools also provide valuable after-school and Saturday programs designed to promote social, emotional, and spiritual development. For example, one school for girls offers after-school and Saturday programs that focus on developing healthy behaviors and attitudes around interpersonal conflict resolution, sexuality, and drug use and continues to develop these themes in its summer program. Also, some Nativity schools sponsor retreats that take the students away from campus at least one long day or a weekend during the regular school year for reflection. For example, the Nativity schools for boys in Boston and Milwaukee hold full-day retreats for their eighth-grade students in the fall.

Field trips support students' social, spiritual, cultural, and academic development as well. For example, seventh-grade students at Bishop Perry School in New Orleans take a three-day civil rights trip to Selma and Birmingham, Alabama, where mission activities are sponsored by the Edmundite Missions Corps. Several schools sponsor annual trips to Washington, DC, for one of their classes. One school holds an annual five-day Outward Bound experience for their eighth graders that one student described as a valuable vehicle for learning to depend on others.

The Nativity school for boys in Milwaukee takes a unique approach to leadership and character development by requiring the sixth-grade boys to join the boy scout troop that is chartered to the school. Most of the seventh and eighth graders decide to continue their involvement in the troop, which meets weekly at the school prior to evening study time and also sponsors an October weekend camping outing. By working closely with the scouting organization, the administration of the school can ensure that the school's mission is served in the scouting program. Leadership and character development are also central themes developed in their summer camp program.

COMMUNITY SERVICE

All of the Nativity schools included community service as a significant component of their educational programs. The motto of the Milwaukee school, "Educating Latino youth for Christian leadership and service," which appears on banners in the school and in most printed materials produced for the school, makes clear the importance of service. Participating in service activities becomes an avenue for students to reflect on local and global social justice issues and understand the importance of a life of service to others.

The kinds of service programs in which Nativity students participate are quite varied. They include raising money from events such as running competitions or golf outings to purchasing goats for a family in Guatemala or sponsoring a child with physical disabilities in Mexico and organizing food drives and baking cookies and breads for local meal programs. Students also work with children in Head Start or other educational or child care settings, visit elderly adults in care facilities, and serve meals at a local meal program or soup kitchen. The Nativity school in Florida requires their graduates in high school to commit several hours of service to their Nativity school through tutoring, office support, or participating in weekend activities with the middle school students.

At a morning assembly in Milwaukee, student members of the Shalom Club described a letter they had written to a major candy manufacturer asking that the company purchase fair trade chocolate for their candy because their present supplier was employing child slave labor in sweatshops. The principal followed the students' presentation by addressing the social injustices of sweatshops. In this way, students acquire a deeper understanding of social justice issues and the experience of taking action to address an injustice.

The president of the Nativity school for girls in New York shared that the time spent talking, making crafts, and singing with residents of a nursing and rehabilitation center is one of the highlights of students' eighth-grade year and the source of fond memories and opportunities for growth. She indicated that the service experience helps the students develop attitudes of respect and reverence for all persons and cited the extent to which the service activities are integrated into the school curriculum and involve significant group reflection related to the service. Teachers carefully guide students in the process of better understanding the realities of economic poverty throughout the world and the roots of this poverty, and encourage them to consider how service might continue to be an integral part of their lives.

COUNSELING

As many educators and researchers can attest, urban children often come to school with numerous life stressors, feelings of inferiority and victimization, poor coping skills, immature behaviors, and a lack of motivation that can find expression in disruptive, and sometimes aggressive, classroom behaviors (Kopetz, Lease, & Warren-Kring, 2006). Considerable expert individual attention is often needed to help urban students adjust to the demands of school.

Recognizing the need to address students' social and emotional difficulties, many of the schools employ, part time in most cases, social workers or other professional counselors who meet with students individually or in small groups to address concerns or issues brought to their attention either by teachers, parents, or students themselves. In my interviews with the counselors, I saw that they were sensitive to the stressful lives that many of the children experience in their homes and the challenges the students confront that include pressures to have sex or become involved in the activities of the street. They also help students work through experiences of the loss of loved ones (often through violence) and the stresses of incarcerated or absent fathers or alcohol and other drug addictions of parents. One of the schools offered a grief support group that several students attended.

To address the many emotional needs and social difficulties that many children face, counselors also offer family counseling and social service advice to parents and workshops for the children. The workshops address such issues as keeping oneself safe outside of school, avoiding harassment and bullying, and making responsible decisions about sexual behaviors and drug use. Students find it beneficial to have some of these topics addressed in multiple contexts.

Counseling needs continue when the students enter the unfamiliar world of selective high schools where they face new academic and social challenges. In many cases, students must learn how to reconcile the wishes of their families with their own desires for a college education, especially when these desires lead them to colleges away from home. Graduate support program directors usually take the first step toward identifying these needs and either providing or arranging for counseling. Often, students in high school return to the Nativity school to talk over difficult matters with a teacher whom they feel close to.

A great deal of the counseling of students takes place informally by teachers. One male teacher described how much he values the one-on-one interactions that the small school size facilitates. These interactions enable him to get to know the students and their families well, along with the students' personal struggles and goals, and allow him to provide some listening or counseling. This sentiment was expressed by several other teachers with whom I spoke as well.

PARENT PROGRAMS

Parent programs help to further the goal of creating a sense of community at the Nativity schools. These programs range from organizing weekend work groups of students and their parents to help clean or spruce up the school building, to involving the parents in planning and preparing meals for special celebrations, to including the parents in off-campus field trips with their children. One of the Boston Nativity schools assigns school cleanup duty to one advisory group each week and then requires the students in the group, along with their parents, to spend a couple of hours at the school on Saturdays to do a more thorough cleaning. Other schools expect parents to contribute a certain number of volunteer hours each month that can be fulfilled with a number of tasks that support the operation of the school.

The Washington, DC school for girls gets the parents involved in the school by hosting mother-daughter social and cultural events and parent nights where outside professionals are brought in to address difficult parenting issues. These sessions tend to be very well attended. Other schools struggle to get many of their parents directly involved in the school and require parents to come to the school at least three times a year to pick up report cards in person and discuss their child's progress. One school sets aside a weekday to require parents of students who were struggling with academics or behaviors to meet with the principal and the child's advisor.

Strong parent participation in the schools was particularly evident in the schools that enrolled students from Latino backgrounds. At one school for girls, where a formal parents' association is in place, special events such as graduation and Thanksgiving are whole-school celebrations for which the parents take the lead in preparing for and catering the celebrations. At the Milwaukee school for boys, parents expressed sincere gratitude for all the teachers and administrators were doing to help their sons with their behavior, spiritual development, motivation for high levels of performance in school, and aspirations for higher education and life success. Parents appreciated the regular contact that the school personnel made with them about positive news and behavioral and academic concerns. They felt that this contact enabled them to follow up with their children and reinforce what the school was trying to do. This group of parents was also quite involved in the school and offered their services with many projects and celebrations. These and other efforts that are undertaken by the schools to involve parents directly and indirectly support the social, academic, and spiritual development of the students. As research has shown, involving parents in the school community benefits the students.

Sports Programs

Although not all Nativity schools have sports teams (due mostly to the lack of outdoor space and gymnasiums), sports and other physical activities serve as a context for the development of leadership and social skills and physical development. Through their sports programs, several schools help the older students provide responsible leadership for the younger ones and the coaches, often volunteer teachers, work hard to encourage sportsmanship, fair play, hard work, and teamwork, as well as skill development.

Physical activity is incorporated into after-school and summer programs. During the school year, students are afforded opportunities to get involved in dance, double-dutch clubs, tennis lessons, and organized team games. Schools also support teams in soccer, basketball, baseball, softball, wrestling, and lacrosse that compete with other school teams. During summer camps, students take part in hiking, canoeing, tubing, horseback riding, and other activities that meet physical developmental needs and contribute to the development of interpersonal skills and community.

I had the opportunity to serve as a volunteer assistant lacrosse coach during the spring of 2004 for the boys' Nativity school in Baltimore and experienced the challenge of helping to support the boys' understanding of teamwork and fair play, as well as fostering the development of skills needed to pass and catch a lacrosse ball. As urban children, these boys had not known the game of lacrosse before enrolling in middle school. As I witnessed the development of their physical skills, I observed other coaches lead the boys to a better understanding of how to involve and support a less-skilled teammate and how to resolve conflicts that come from competition on the practice field and during games, a practice that I engaged in as well. In addition, I also observed and became involved in efforts to encourage the boys when their play fell short of their expectations.

PEOPLE AND RELATIONSHIPS

Perhaps the single most important contribution to the students' social, emotional, moral, and spiritual development is the quality of the teachers and administrators with whom the students come into regular contact through the school program. Consistently across the schools, students, alumni, and parents sang the praises of the staff that was supportive and caring and contributed much to the perception nearly all had of the school as a family. Invariably, students reported that there was at least one adult whom they felt comfortable approaching to discuss personal problems and challenges. Although it was not uncommon to hear students complain that some teachers were too strict, these same students also recognized how supportive and caring these teachers were.

Several alumni also acknowledged the importance of the relationships with teachers and other students while at the school and that continue to be a part of their lives as high school students. These graduates often come back to their Nativity schools to seek academic assistance, to meet up with classmates, or to talk over a personal problem with a teacher they had come to trust. Graduates I interviewed also expressed gratitude for Nativity teachers who sought them out to encourage them and provide consistent support that helped them to achieve and establish sound goals for their futures. However, because these relationships with teachers are so important to students' social and emotional development, students and a few administrators and teachers acknowledged that the short-term employment of the volunteer teachers causes difficulties for some students who have trouble trusting adults. In order to address this issue, school personnel help students understand the nature of the volunteer teacher program and most schools have been able to keep a core of teachers and administrators on staff for several years.

In all the Nativity schools I visited, I found the attention that the schools paid to students' social, emotional, moral, and spiritual developmental needs to be exceptional and effective, at least for the students and graduates I was able to meet and speak with. I would suggest that the level of success that the schools clearly experienced in addressing these needs could not be realized if these schools were much larger. Although the kinds of programs differ somewhat from school to school, they are certainly consistent with the mission of the Nativity network of schools and that of each individual school. The graduate support program sponsored by each of the schools also helps to support graduates' continued development in these important areas by maintaining close personal relationships with graduates, offering counseling and tutoring when needed, and providing opportunities for graduates to return to the school to tutor and interact with current students. I recall how one Nativity school graduate appreciated the opportunity to return to the school and obtain some assistance from her middle school English teacher with her high school courses.

TEACHER PREPARATION

In order to be effective models and translators of the spiritual and social goals of the school for students, teachers must be educated properly in the school's mission and goals and given opportunities for their own spiritual development and reflection. Without exception, this education is the first priority for the teaching workshops that prepare the teachers for the fall semester. In addition, training and mentoring throughout the school year also help to keep teachers focused on the mission of the school.

Training in the school's mission, goals, and practices is most important for volunteer teachers who commit themselves to only two years of service to the schools. The teacher handbooks provided by the schools contain the mission statement and information to help teachers contribute to carrying out that mission. Most volunteer teachers also live in community settings where regular group reflections are led by one of the more experienced volunteers, a full-time member of the staff, or representative of the religious organization that sponsors the school. Because the teachers can feel overwhelmed and inadequate when dealing with struggling urban students (Delpit, 2006a), they must take advantage of opportunities for meeting their own spiritual and emotional needs.

SIX

Instruction and Instructional Quality in Nativity Schools

MAINTAINING A HIGHLY effective teaching staff is one of the greatest challenges and shortcomings facing urban public schools. A great deal of literature has either directly described the difficulties teachers experience in urban classrooms or indirectly addressed them by citing statistics about the high incidence of urban teacher attrition. The violence or perceived threat of violence in urban schools and the surrounding neighborhoods, along with a lack of adequate curriculum materials and teaching assignments that tend to place inexperienced teachers with the most educationally challenged (and challenging) students, contribute to considerable teacher turnover (Smith & Smith, 2006). In addition, studies (Ingersoll, 2001) show that student discipline problems, a lack of student motivation to learn, and inadequate administrative support also contribute to teacher turnover. Clearly, many urban teachers often feel overwhelmed, undervalued, and ineffective (Delpit, 2006a; Murrell, 2008) because of the difficult challenges they face.

The vast majority of Nativity school teachers, on the other hand, love teaching their students and have plenty of support to be effective in the classroom. These teachers are young adults fresh out of college, mid-career professionals with several years of urban public school teaching experience, members of religious congregations who have taught many years in parochial schools, and middle-aged career changers.

In this chapter, I take a careful look at the strengths and weaknesses of the teaching staffs at Nativity schools and evaluate the extent to which volunteer teachers, who are used to varying extents in the schools, are successful at managing their classrooms and providing effective instruction. In addition, understanding that most Nativity schools are very successful at helping students achieve impressive academic gains, I examine how the schools utilize experienced and volunteer teachers effectively. To this end, I present data on teachers' self-perceptions of their effectiveness and challenges, students' perceptions of the quality of the learning climate in classes taught by experienced and volunteer teachers, and classroom observation data, along with information on the ways in which teachers are prepared and mentored. I show that volunteer teachers contribute much to the academic and social-emotional growth of Nativity students and address effective ways of making use of them.

THE IMPORTANCE OF TEACHER QUALITY

Some educators and educational researchers have made it clear that urban children, like suburban and rural children, are quite capable of high levels of academic learning and performance. They also insist that, with the proper conditions and effective approaches to instruction, teachers can and do make a difference in urban students' levels of success (e.g., Delpit, 2006a). Smaller, more personalized urban secondary schools provide a context for improved teaching and learning, although they usually demand a great deal of time and energy from teachers that can drain their inner resources and contribute to burnout (Keller, 2007).

Despite the difficulties of maintaining an effective teaching staff in urban schools, research findings show clearly and unequivocally that the better the instructional quality in a classroom, the better students learn (e.g., Cochran-Smith, 2003; Kaplan & Owings, 2001; Maryland State Department of Education, 2003). Effective teaching requires teachers to have an excellent command of their subject matter as well as a sensitive understanding of their students that enables them to motivate the students and guide their learning. Since Nativity schools are quite successful in advancing student learning and improving students' academic skills, one would expect them to be staffed with a core of highly effective teachers.

THE USE OF VOLUNTEER TEACHERS

The percentage of volunteer faculty in the Nativity schools examined in this study ranged from 13 to 71 percent of the teaching staff (see Table A.2). On the average, 46 percent of teachers in the Nativity schools studied were first- or second-year volunteers hired through Americorps and other volunteer organizations such as Jesuit Volunteer Corps and Edmundite Mission Volunteers. These teachers, nearly all of whom are recent college graduates with four-year degrees, are expected to commit themselves to two years of service in their schools. Their compensation consists of housing, health insurance, and meals that are provided by the schools along with a modest monthly stipend and a tuition allowance provided by Americorps or either the umbrella volunteer organization or the school. Most volunteers live in modest community housing with other volunteers where they also participate in group reflection activities together that are designed for their professional, personal, and spiritual growth and development.

Some influential educational researchers (e.g., Darling-Hammond, 2000) have suggested that the practice of employing volunteer teachers, such as those hired by Teach for America, Americorps, and other volunteer organizations, fails students placed at risk because the teachers lack the preparation to be as effective as those considered highly qualified (i.e., those who possess full certification and a major in their teaching area). Classroom experience is also very important as teacher effectiveness seems to peak at about five years of classroom teaching experience (Darling-Hammond, 2000). Is it possible, then, that employing volunteer teachers can be a disservice to the Nativity school children who are considered at risk?

In research that more directly addresses the effect on student learning of employing uncertified and inexperienced teachers through Teach for America (TFA), Laczko-Kerr and Berliner (2002) found that elementary school students taught by TFA men and women performed more poorly on standardized tests than did students taught by certified teachers in similar settings. However, other research (Decker, Mayer, & Glazerman, 2004; Raymond, Fletcher, & Luque, 2001) has shown that TFA volunteers have positive effects on student learning. For example, the study conducted by Decker et al., which compared TFA teachers with novice trained controls in low-income schools in six school districts, found higher math achievement gains for students instructed by TFA teachers when compared to students taught by controls, even though TFA teachers entered their teaching placements having had less previous classroom experience than novice control teachers.

An important aspect of the learning experiences of Nativity students that must be considered in this analysis is the out-of-class tutoring and homework assistance provided by volunteer teachers, and, in some cases, community volunteers, during the long day that students spend in the schools. In some Nativity schools, particularly those that have a high percentage of volunteer teachers on staff, students benefit from the one-on-one assistance offered by volunteer teachers. Such tutoring and homework assistance provide students with added time devoted to learning activities that is not present in most public and private middle schools, although many alternative programs that have appeared in recent years, such as the Knowledge Is Power Program (KIPP), incorporate an added tutoring and study feature as part of their required school program. However, programs such as KIPP do not have the low student–teacher ratios that having volunteer teachers affords.

TEACHER SELF-PERCEPTIONS OF
INSTRUCTIONAL PRACTICES AND EFFECTIVENESS

Teachers completed questionnaire items that addressed their perceptions of their own performance and challenges in the classroom. For this study, I conducted several analyses to compare differences in these perceptions for experienced and certified teachers versus noncertified, volunteer teachers that are reported in detail elsewhere (Fenzel & Flippen, 2006). To summarize these findings, volunteer teachers reported that they needed to spend class time disciplining students to a greater extent than did full-time, experienced teachers and expressed the view that student misbehavior was more of a problem. Furthermore, volunteer teachers reported a lower level of satisfaction with the quality of their teaching and with their success at engaging very difficult and unmotivated students, and reported that they engaged students less often in class activities. I also compared the perceptions of first- and second-year volunteer teachers to see what difference, if any, a year of experience makes for volunteers. Results showed that second-year teachers reported a significantly higher level of satisfaction with the quality of their teaching and greater success engaging difficult and unmotivated students.

I conducted additional analyses to determine if certification status, independent of years of teaching experience, mattered with respect to these perceptions. These results showed that certified teachers reported greater success in engaging difficult and unmotivated students and a greater likelihood of employing classroom learning activities that involved the students (Fenzel & Flippen, 2006).

These results furnish some evidence that both experience and certification matter, at least as far as teachers' perceptions of their competence in the classroom are concerned. That is, teachers find that both the classroom experience and the learning involved in obtaining certification enable them to engage the more challenging students better and to more effectively facilitate learning that actively engages students in the process. Because these findings represent only teachers' self-perceptions, more data were important to examine with respect to the importance of teacher certification and experience to the academic success and social development of Nativity schoolchildren.

STUDENT PERCEPTIONS OF TEACHER EFFECTIVENESS

Perhaps a more objective assessment of the instructional quality and classroom management skills of more experienced teachers when compared with volunteer teachers can be found in the data analyzed from questionnaires completed by 398 students who assessed the climate of their language arts (or English) and mathematics classes taught by either experienced full-time or volunteer teachers. (Whether a given child's teacher was a volunteer or full-time, experienced teacher was determined from information on teacher assignments provided by each school. In some cases the teacher could not be identified.) Results showed that students perceived the climate of the mathematics classes and language arts classes as being more supportive and task oriented when the instructor was an experienced full-time teacher than when he or she was an inexperienced volunteer (see Fenzel & Flippen, 2006).

CLASSROOM OBSERVATIONS AND INTERVIEWS WITH TEACHERS, PRINCIPALS, AND STUDENTS

Using a modified version of the Classroom Environment Scale (CES; Moos & Trickett, 1987), I recorded the extent to which teachers exhibited behaviors associated with a supportive and task-oriented classroom climate during extended observations of twenty-five classes. At the time of the observation I did not always know whether the teacher was a full-time, experienced teacher or a volunteer. Results showed that classes conducted by volunteer teachers, especially those in their first year of teaching, were characterized by significantly lower levels of student involvement, teacher control, and task orientation, as compared to the classes taught by experienced full-time teachers. Differences with respect to order and organization and teacher support also favored experienced teachers, although these differences did not achieve statistical significance.

Qualitative data I recorded during these and other class observations inform and corroborate the findings of the CES analyses and teacher and student questionnaire responses. For example, a first-year volunteer teacher conducting a science lab exercise for twelve girls working in teams of three seemed to be managing students' behaviors well as they engaged in the activities of the lab. I observed students weighing objects and recording data and talking with one another about what they were doing. However, I noticed that several girls in the back of the room were recording data incorrectly and conducting incorrect mathematical calculations. The teacher failed to monitor the activities of two of the groups or to recognize that some of the students were not grasping the concepts the activity was designed for them to learn. At another school, a first-year teacher, who had asked students to raise their hands and be acknowledged before answering his questions, repeatedly permitted violations of this requirement and used a considerable amount of class time to address misbehavior of the group of eight students, as well as that of individual students. I observed several other first-year volunteers struggle with classroom management as well. On the other hand, a first-year volunteer math teacher at one school, who happened to be certified, had very good control of a class of fourteen boys in which several students asked questions about the content of the teacher's presentation, although three or four boys appeared to be disengaged in the lesson for part of the class. In classes conducted by experienced full-time teachers, and most second-year volunteers, instruction was generally more varied and teacher control, student engagement, and time on task were of higher quality when compared to first-year volunteers' classes. One area for which only a small difference was found favoring experienced teachers over inexperienced teachers was on the level of support that teachers gave students during class time.

FINDINGS FROM INTERVIEWS

In interviews with experienced and volunteer teachers and school administrators, the most frequently cited difficulty volunteer teachers faced was the management of student behavior in the classroom. On the other hand, principals were in unanimous agreement about the benefits that young adult volunteers brought to the school in terms of their heightened motivation to help students, their high energy levels, and their commitment to working long hours. Because of the struggles faced by four first-year volunteer teachers at one school during the previous year when they were given immediate responsibility for several classes each day, the principal changed the manner in which she utilized the two first-year volunteers during the time of the present study by gradually increasing their classroom responsibilities as the school year progressed; their competencies subsequently improved. In addition, the principal increased the amount of time she spent in coaching the volunteer teachers.

In schools where first-year volunteer teachers taught fewer hours in the classroom, they tutored individual or small groups of students and were assigned to afternoon and evening study hall supervision, in addition to afternoon sports or activity supervision or coaching duties. In most schools, second-year volunteers logged more classroom teaching hours than first-years did. All principals indicated that the volunteer teachers were crucial to the success of their schools because of the important duties they performed, such as tutoring and monitoring after-school athletic and arts programs, for which the schools could not afford to hire certified, experienced teachers.

In focus group interviews with students, two main themes emerged with respect to the volunteer teachers. Students generally expressed disappointment that the volunteer teachers left the school after students got to know them for only one or two years. Much more so, however, students expressed widespread appreciation for and benefit from the genuine personal concern and interest that the volunteer teachers, as well as full-time teachers and administrators, showed them. In particular, students' comments consistently indicated that they appreciated the volunteer teachers being available for academic help and that nearly all teachers listened to them and showed that they cared.

Several Nativity school graduates cited a particular teacher whom they found especially helpful to them and with whom they developed close friendships. Because these relationships developed over time, they tended to be with teachers who stayed at the Nativity school for several years. These graduates indicated how the teachers tended to approach them with encouragement and indicated a willingness to listen to them as the students addressed home problems or learning struggles. These teachers also continued to support the students academically and emotionally through their high school, and into their college, years.

TEST SCORE DATA AND TEACHER EFFECTIVENESS

Considering the research, primarily in conjunction with the assessments of the Teach for America program, that examined the relation between teacher volunteer status or level of experience and students' scores on standardized tests, I also conducted some school-level analyses. Although the number of schools for which test score data were available (only eight) was small, one interesting finding emerged. This analysis showed a significant positive correlation ($\rho = .84$, $p = .005$) between the percentage of volunteer teachers on staff and the *gain* in students' standardized test scores in mathematics (assessed in terms of the percentage of students in the school who had gained the equivalent of one grade level or more per year of attendance). The correlation between the percentage of volunteer teachers on staff and reading achievement gains was also positive ($\rho = .42$) but not statistically significant. No significant correlations were found between student achievement gains and either the size of the teaching staff or the student–teacher ratio in the schools.

The finding that having more volunteer teachers in the school is related to greater student achievement gains seems to be inconsistent with the findings of studies that show that having students taught by TFA volunteers undermines student academic performance. However, the present finding reflects a phenomenon present in Nativity schools that is not found in most public and private middle schools. In Nativity schools, the amount of time during which students participate in learning activities is increased on a daily basis by the inclusion of after-school tutoring and homework assistance. These homework and tutoring periods, staffed mostly by volunteer teachers (and also by unpaid volunteers, many of whom are college and high school students), are held for an average of two hours each day, four days a week (and on Saturdays for students who have not completed their weekly assignments in many schools). The presence of several volunteer teachers increases the amount of individual attention and academic assistance Nativity students receive from intelligent college graduates who haven't yet developed the skills needed to teach groups of students in formal classes effectively. In addition, the presence of volunteer teachers enables schools to provide struggling students with individualized instruction, such as in reading and math, during regular school hours.

A look at one of the highest performing Nativity schools, a coeducational school in New England, provides an illustration of how volunteer teachers are used effectively to boost student achievement. This school has an enrollment of eighty-one students, forty boys and forty-one girls, in grades five through eight, and a staff of seven experienced professional teachers and eleven volunteer teachers (six first-year and five second-year). In the first standardized testing, administered to students in May of the fifth-grade year, 36 percent of students tested at or above grade level in reading and 40 percent at or above grade level in math. For the class that graduated in 2004, 53 percent tested at or above grade level in both reading and math at the May seventh-grade testing. Other analyses showed that nearly 80 percent of the students at the school improved the equivalent of one or more grade levels per year in reading and 66 percent in math between fifth and seventh grade. A feature that makes this school unique, even among Nativity schools, is that most students are selected for admission by lottery (among those families that qualify for the federal free or reduced meal program) and four students are selected each year from the foster-care system. Volunteer instructors teach two classes each day, coach a sport or supervise an activity during the afternoon activity period, supervise two evening study halls each week, and take part in one additional duty (usually a committee assignment).

The Nativity school that has the largest percentage of volunteer teachers on its faculty is another example of how the volunteers are used effectively. In this school, where over 80 percent of the students arrive in fifth or sixth grade testing below grade level and nearly all graduate testing at or above grade level and attend high-quality private or public high schools (as reported by the school's principal; actual test scores were not provided), structures are in place to help students obtain the maximum benefit from the educational program. First, volunteers teach only in areas that correspond to their undergraduate college major and are offered a position only after they have spent a day at the school and have taught a class during their visit. Candidates have to show the teaching and administrative staff that they have at least the *potential* to be an effective teacher of urban middle school boys, the desire to work with urban boys, and a commitment to the Jesuit-influenced ideals of social justice in action.

The scheduling of classes supports the development of volunteer teachers at this school. For example, all reading and English/language arts classes are taught during the first two periods of the day, freeing up these teachers in the afternoon to plan classes together and to help one another out with techniques they find effective in the classroom. In addition, all teachers' desks are located in one large faculty room that adjoins the principal's office, a situation that promotes collegial problem solving and support. Regular meetings are held by grade level as well so that teachers are aware of any particular student issues that need to be addressed.

The size of the volunteer staff at this all-boys school makes it possible for many classes to be either team-taught or for a class of fourteen to sixteen boys to be divided up into two or three smaller groups for instruction. Students with special needs can then receive the kind of help they require to support their academic development.

VOLUNTEER TEACHER
PREPARATION AND DEVELOPMENT

Nativity schools employ a variety of means to ensure volunteer teacher success. In addition to orienting the new teachers to the mission of the school and the expectations of their position, Nativity administrators give them an initial brief course in lesson planning, teaching methods, and classroom management. This late-summer orientation lasts only five to ten days and tends to leave at least some volunteers anxious about meeting the students and conducting a class for the first time. In a small number of schools, volunteer teachers are expected to take part in the summer camp program prior to the beginning of their fall teaching assignment, which helps them get to know the students and begin to feel comfortable in the Nativity environment.

Some schools are blessed by having exceptionally gifted and highly trained instructional leaders who can educate new teachers on current approaches to lesson planning and effective instructional techniques. Other schools are able to hire the services of teacher education faculty or doctoral students from local colleges or universities to provide initial training, as well as follow-up assistance.

Volunteer teachers receive ongoing support and mentoring at all Nativity schools from a combination of mentor or master teachers, principals, and consultants. At the Baltimore boys' school, I attended one of the weekly meetings of volunteer faculty with a part-time, on-site consultant at which she addressed particular difficulties faced in the classroom that the teachers reported. The atmosphere of the meeting was respectful, professional, and supportive and the teachers reported that they found the sessions very helpful. At the girls' school in Manhattan, volunteer teachers were blessed by having a principal who held extremely helpful weekly mentoring sessions with each volunteer, a practice that was utilized in other Nativity schools as well. In some schools, the mentoring structure was less formalized, but most volunteer teachers indicated that they felt that they could approach full-time teachers and principals with questions or concerns. Volunteers generally were more pleased with situations in which the mentoring function was more structured.

Another component of the professional development of Nativity volunteer teachers at most schools was the provision and encouragement of graduate study in education at a local college or university. In many cases, Nativity schools have formed partnerships with area colleges or universities that enable teachers to pursue graduate studies at little or no cost. Volunteer teachers were also presented the opportunity to observe experienced teachers' classes or classes at other schools and attend workshops and retreats designed to improve instruction.

Many Nativity schools view the development of volunteer teachers as a part of the mission of the school. To that end, they take seriously the importance of providing volunteer teachers with opportunities to develop spiritually as well as professionally. Part of this function involves housing the volunteer faculty together in the community and providing educational and spiritual group reflection sessions on a regular basis. Led by spiritual directors trained in the charism of the religious order that operates the school, for example the Jesuits or the Edmundites, these directors provide volunteers with opportunities to address their experiences and challenges with others from a spiritual, and sometimes a more practical, perspective.

The teacher intern program at Mother Caroline Academy in Boston is certainly among the best of any I learned about as I conducted this study. The two-week program prior to the opening of the school year begins with an orientation to the mission, procedures, and organization of the school and the Educational Center, the school's expectations of its teachers, students, and parents, and an introduction to the curriculum. Four days are spent with members of the education faculty at a nearby college that focus on unit planning, lesson plan construction, classroom management, and other fundamentals of effective teaching. Regular meetings with and observations by master teachers and an administrator follow during the school year. In addition, the structure of the teachers' office space, along with the leadership of the master teachers and members of the administration provide an excellent context for consultation and group problem solving. Without question, an atmosphere of care, mutual support, and teamwork was strong among the staff.

SELECTED TEACHER PROFILES

To put more of a human face on the committed men and women who teach the Nativity students, I describe in this section the background and characteristics of four teachers in four different schools and summarize an observation I conducted of one of each teacher's classes. In some ways, these teachers reflect common characteristics of a majority of the Nativity teachers, yet they also demonstrate the diversity present among them. The first individual was a master teacher at the Boston school for girls, the second a second-year intern at the Baltimore school for boys, the third a second-year full-time but not-yet-certified teacher at Baltimore's coed school, and the fourth a first-year intern at the school for boys in New Orleans. Only the St. Ignatius intern is a person of color.

When I met with Colleen, she was in her third year of full-time teaching at Mother Caroline Academy, having first served for two years as a volunteer intern there and one year as a certified teacher in a Boston-area public school after the completion of her master's degree in elementary education. In keeping with the school's desire to minimize the number of teachers that the fifth-grade students have for instruction, Colleen taught fifth-grade language arts (a double period), math, and study skills and served as the homeroom teacher. As one of two master teachers she helped to conduct the summer training for the interns and continued to observe their teaching periodically and lead weekly grade-level faculty meetings. A graduate of a New England Jesuit college, she is committed to the social justice mission of the school to educate students living in economic poverty for leadership and service.

My observation of her class demonstrated to me that she is indeed a masterful teacher. In the language arts class, which was addressing subject–verb agreement, the girls were engaged in a whole class question-and-answer activity, completed worksheets on their own, compared their answers with a partner, read out their answers when called on, and asked questions of the teacher. After Colleen distributed a new homework assignment on the topic, she had the students make a speedy transition to a new topic as she directed them to take out the novel they were reading and promptly began to ask a number of Why questions about the activities of the characters in the book. She also asked students to address parallels between the lives of the characters to the roles played by members of their own families. In calling on students, Colleen used popsicle sticks on which their names were written and selected sticks at random. Throughout the lesson, the students were engaged and the teacher demonstrated a high level of respect as she challenged them to think critically and creatively.

Rory was a second-year intern who was recruited at a career fair by the headmaster at St. Ignatius Loyola Academy in Baltimore. An African American and Jesuit college graduate, Rory was involved in community service and worked with urban high school students placed at risk while in college. At the time of my visit, he was teaching three or four science classes each day within a work day that began at 7 A.M. and extended until about 5:30 P.M. and was planning a science outing for students to the Chesapeake Bay. He served as the coordinator of the volunteer teachers with whom he lived in a row house just around the corner from the school and led regularly scheduled reflection activities that helped the volunteers process their teaching experiences in light of the Jesuit mission of the school. He was also pursuing a master's degree in educational administration at the time. As of the fall of 2008, Rory was returning to St. Ignatius as a full-time administrator with some teaching responsibilities. He expects to complete his M.Ed. in educational leadership in the spring of 2009.

I found the quality of Rory's teaching to be excellent. As the seventh-grade students entered his science room, he greeted each boy with a Mr.

before his surname and directed the students to complete a *Do Now* assignment that was waiting for them at their desks. His interactions with the students were friendly with a manner that could be described as respectfully assertive, or what Delpit (2006b) identified as authoritative, and students moved from one activity to the next smoothly. His class was well prepared with a skeletal plan for the period displayed on the side board. His lesson on steps in the food chain was informative and related to the students' upcoming Chesapeake Bay project. He calmly and consistently insisted on students raising their hands and waiting to be called on for responses. All fourteen boys in the class were attentive and engaged.

A second-year full-time teacher at Mother Seton Academy in Baltimore, Mark came to the school a few months after graduating from a Jesuit college with a major in classics and a minor in Catholic studies. Although he had no prior classroom teaching experience, his experience with tutoring urban children in an after-school program convinced him to pursue a teaching position at the school as he studied for his master's degree and certification. He was teaching six classes a day in social studies and science (with the latter presenting him with considerable challenges at first), supervising one late-afternoon homework club session a week, and helping to start a school newspaper. Even on days when he was not supervising homework time he would stay at the school helping students, planning classes, or grading papers until 5 P.M. or so. In addition, his planning periods were often spent helping students.

In my interview with him, Mark demonstrated remarkable insight into methods of effective instruction and understanding of principles of student cognitive and social-emotional development. For example, he underscored the importance of encouraging and promoting critical thinking and the expression of informed opinion from his students as he acknowledged the need to help them acquire basic historical and geographic knowledge that they lacked. He led students in his social studies classes in discussions of how a society and its government is structured and functions and issues of power, class, and racism. He noted how remarkably students grew during the course of a year at the school in their social skills, including conflict resolution skills, and in taking responsibility for their learning. A need he identified as crucial was for more counseling services to help students with significant emotional difficulties and stress stemming from troubled family situations.

His eighth-grade science class that I observed was well organized and the students were attentive and engaged throughout the lesson on faults and earthquakes, despite the late afternoon hour and a warm room. Mark began the lesson by asking the ten boys seated in a U-shape arrangement of desks to tell him about what they learned the day before, calling out a student's name and simultaneously passing a soft rubber ball to him. The pace of the question-and-answer session was quick with the ball being passed back and forth between teacher and student. At the end of this introductory activity, Mark asked students to take out their homework and science notebooks and to complete an assignment that was posted on the overhead projector as he went around the room to check each student's homework. Mark appeared confident, respectful, focused, and in control throughout the lesson.

One of the particularly effective first-year volunteer teachers was a Caucasian man who possessed the only teaching certificate among the volunteers. John, a graduate of a small midwestern Catholic college, had taken part in a spring break service experience in Alabama while in college that was overseen by the religious group that sponsored his New Orleans Nativity school. He taught two math classes a day, each of which extended for one hundred minutes (and fifty minutes on Fridays), and helped students during the afternoon study hall that ran from 3:15 until 5 P.M. He also worked with alumni in high school who came to the school for math assistance. Because of the wide range of math ability among his students, he often used cooperative learning activities in heterogeneous groups in which more talented students could assist struggling students with difficult concepts.

Although he described how classroom management was a challenge for him, even with his student teaching experience, his eighth-grade math class that I observed was very well managed, despite the students' excitement about a championship basketball game that had been rescheduled for that afternoon. Students entered his classroom and settled themselves quickly when the bell rang. John laid out the schedule for the day that called for students to take part in a computer exercise in the computer lab next door. In the lab, he circulated well among the fifteen students, answering their questions and occasionally reminding students to maintain quiet.

CONCLUSIONS ABOUT TEACHERS AND INSTRUCTION IN NATIVITY SCHOOLS

The use of volunteer teachers at Nativity schools certainly seems to contribute positively to student success, despite the difficulties that many first-year teachers have with classroom management. What then do we make of the success of the volunteer teacher program at the Nativity schools in light of the research that insists that every teacher of urban children placed at risk be highly qualified? Do the findings of this study contradict the conclusions drawn by highly regarded teacher education researchers about the importance of having only highly qualified teachers for urban children placed at risk?

I think that answers to these questions must take into consideration the unique context of Nativity schools with respect to their small size, their students who share at least somewhat of a desire to succeed and usually have adequate support at home to do so, and the spiritual orientation and sound organization of the Nativity schools that attracts volunteer teachers who are well educated, intelligent college graduates committed to the social justice mission of improving the education of urban children at risk. In order to make effective use of volunteer teachers in larger public schools, school administrators and teachers must be willing to provide adequate mentoring and move the volunteers into classroom teaching as their skills develop. Nothing would be gained by assigning inexperienced volunteers classes of twenty-five or more students on the first day of school. Starting the volunteers with opportunities for tutoring, team teaching, small-group instruction, along with graduate courses in education, can help them grow into effective teachers.

Volunteer teachers have been a part of the Nativity school model ever since the opening of the first Nativity school in 1971. Results of the present study suggest that the benefits of employing the volunteers for classroom instruction and tutoring far outweigh the costs. The principal of the Boston school for boys introduced an important perspective that explains why the volunteer teacher program works in Nativity schools. It is effective, in part, because the schools where the volunteers teach are small enough for them to receive effective mentoring, the administrators are highly qualified instructional leaders who understand urban children placed at risk, and the students are relatively similar in their educational needs. The surprising correlation found in the present analysis between the relative size of the volunteer faculty and student standardized test score performance can be understood in the context of the nature of Nativity schools that are small with small groups of students for instruction and the use of volunteer teachers to reduce the size of student groups even further for instruction. Schools with large numbers of volunteer teachers are also able to pair a first-year teacher with a second-year teacher in team-teaching arrangements that help the more inexperienced teachers learn the ropes of managing a classroom and delivering a lesson without shortchanging the students' educational experience.

The volunteers also bring something to the Nativity schools that cannot be found in other schools in that they are available to the students for ten to twelve hours a day at least four days a week as well as on Saturdays and during the summer sessions. Although many students dislike seeing these teachers leave after two years, the volunteers give an incredible amount of themselves to the students. The students recognize their high energy levels, enthusiasm, and genuine interest in and care for them, factors that research (Storz & Nestor, 2008; Wilson & Corbett, 2001) clearly shows impact student learning. Although they come to the schools not fully understanding what they have gotten themselves into, the teachers bring such an exceptional level of commitment to social justice in education that this seems to make up, to some extent, for their lack of experience. Many volunteer teachers end up continuing in their schools as full-time certified teachers. A few have even proceeded to contribute to the founding of other Nativity schools or to serve in administrative roles in the schools.

There is also something to be said for the quality of the undergraduate college educations that these volunteers receive prior to their teaching, with degrees from prestigious universities and majors in the subject areas they teach. There is some evidence that teachers' verbal ability contributes to student achievement (Abell Foundation, 2001; Darling-Hammond, 2002), although other factors related to teachers' capabilities are certainly more influential. However, combined with their energy and levels of commitment to their work, the intellectual capabilities of the volunteers must be considered in evaluating the benefits they bring.

Of course, a few Nativity schools have chosen to reduce their dependence on volunteer teachers for classroom teaching duties and have moved toward the hiring of experienced and certified teachers almost exclusively for classroom instruction and the use of volunteers for tutoring and other support functions. This practice can be cost effective in schools where some of the teachers are members of religious communities but, with the small and declining numbers of adults in religious life available for teaching duties, these schools may not be able to afford a full-time certified teaching staff and still provide small classes for instruction for long. The principal of the Boston all-boys school estimated that he would need to hire six full-time teachers to take the place of his eleven volunteer teachers, and even then the school would not have the coverage of study halls and opportunities for individualized instruction that it has currently.

As the statistics from this study show, most Nativity schools face the same challenges that other urban schools do with respect to a lack of teachers from racial/ethnic, economic, and social backgrounds similar to those of the students. Recruiting efforts are directed specifically at hiring faculty with whom students can identify with some success. Administrators at nearly all of the schools reflected on the difficulties they have even finding candidates of color to recruit. Still, some of the schools have done a remarkable job of hiring teachers of color. At the Milwaukee school, one of the Spanish teachers was recruited by the school president when he was on a trip to Mexico.

The findings from this research suggest that intelligent, well-educated, energetic, and committed young adults provide a resource that can be used to improve urban education in settings other than Nativity schools. Unfortunately, the requirements put forth by state departments of education, especially with the challenges presented by the No Child Left Behind legislation, as well as tight budgets, prohibit most public urban schools from hiring such promising individuals in roles that can prove beneficial for children placed at risk. Public and parochial urban schools whose students are placed at risk would benefit from hiring young college graduates through Americorps or similar programs for after-school programs and school-day tutoring or small-group instruction. I believe that these young adults who have an interest in working with urban children would be attracted to well-organized programs that would place them in schools where they felt they could make a substantial contribution. Also, because volunteer teachers serve only two years in a school, they may well be able to maintain a level of enthusiasm and drive that begins to wane for teachers who work long days for several years in challenging urban schools.

The most important way to examine the issue of the use of volunteer teachers is not whether schools should or should not employ them. Volunteer teachers can and do make extremely valuable contributions to student learning and development. Although I would not go so far as Ness (2004) did in her examination of the Teach for America program that what the inexperienced teachers of students placed at risk "lack in formal training and pedagogical theory they make up for in compassion, motivation, and energy" (p. 198), I would suggest that such dispositions certainly contribute much to a teacher's effectiveness. At the same time, these dispositions are not enough as well-intentioned volunteer teachers thrown into a classroom without mentoring and an adequate set of tools for instruction and classroom management are not going to contribute much to student learning. The use of volunteer teachers must be a part of a larger plan for effective education that includes a strong standards-based curriculum, expert teachers, and knowledgeable school administrators who have the time and expertise to provide much-needed ongoing mentoring. Volunteer teacher programs must be well organized and the teachers must be given the opportunities to learn and receive professional and emotional support.

Overall, the instructional quality in Nativity schools is quite good because teachers and administrators work together as a team. Plenty of time is set aside for grade-level and content-area meetings, observations, and formal and informal consultations and the spirit of cooperation among the staffs is enviable. The small size of the Nativity schools also enables teachers to work in close proximity to one another. In addition, the group living situation provided for volunteers enables them to offer each other support and to have a context for self-reflection, a sentiment echoed by Ness (2004) with respect to the Teach for America program.

SEVEN

Costs, Funding, and Governance

BECAUSE NATIVITY SCHOOLS provide an education comparable in quality to that in elite private and parochial schools and must prepare their students to succeed academically and socially in challenging high school programs, they require the quality facilities and staff needed to do so. In addition, because of their commitment to small class sizes for instruction and the need to hire quality teachers and administrators to staff their extensive programs, the cost to educate each student is bound to exceed that of public schools, especially urban public schools, to a considerable degree. In order to be successful, Nativity schools must have well-organized and effective fund raising programs, although some variation in the effectiveness of these programs exists.

As this chapter shows, Nativity schools vary in their funding needs and in the ways in which they seek funding to meet annual operating expenses, as well as in the levels of success they have in securing funds. All Nativity schools solicit private and corporate gifts and foundation support in their development programs. For some schools, the success of their fund-raising efforts affects the scope and quality of the programs they provide.

PROGRAM EXPENSES

Estimates of the cost per student to operate the Nativity schools included in this study ranged from a low of approximately $8,000 per student at the grade 5–8 school for boys in New Orleans to as high as $19,000 per student at a coeducational grade 5–8 school in Boston that offers a wide range of services to its students. Differences in the costs per student for the schools exist because of a number of factors, including differences in physical plant costs, the number of salaried professionals, and the services and programs offered, including the after-school and summer programs. Also, some schools include in their budgets funds to provide support for graduates' high school tuitions.

The average cost per student among the eleven Nativity schools included in this study for all programs except graduate support was approximately $14,000 for the 2003–2004 academic year.

For a small number of schools, the school program comprises one part of a larger effort that also provides tutoring for younger children or adult educational programs, or both, such as is the case for the girls' school in Boston that was a part of this study. This school also operated an adult education program and an after-school program for elementary school students in their multiuse building. In another case, the president of the New York City boys' school also served as president for two other Nativity schools and the development office located at this school served all three of the schools that operate under the authority of this president. In these cases, development, some administrative, and other costs are shared among several programs or schools. Most of the schools, however, operate completely independently of other schools and programs.

Capital Expenses

Debt service for the school building also accounts for some differences in the schools' operating costs. Some of the schools, which have invested in new or renovated buildings, have loan payments that figure into the annual costs while other schools have little or no rent or mortgage expense because they operate in donated space or space that was completely paid for through effective capital campaigns. Some schools reported outstanding fund-raising success to support capital projects.

Several schools were also facing the costs of needing to update their computer labs in order to help their students become better prepared for the technology challenges of selective high schools. Schools already operating in small buildings faced the additional challenge of providing library space and an adequate collection of literary materials, and several schools lacked space for indoor sports activities as well. These factors were contributing to the efforts of some schools to attempt to purchase and renovate a larger building.

Staffing

The level of a school's staffing costs is related in part to the nature of the school's teaching staff as it costs three times as much, or more, to employ a certified full-time teacher as it does to employ a volunteer teacher, although a volunteer teacher usually works longer hours at the school than a full-time teacher does. In addition, some schools have faculty and administrators who are members of religious orders of men or women whose congregations donate their services to the schools. Also, some schools are fortunate to have retired educators and other members of the community serve the school in a volunteer capacity. For example, one of the schools had a full-time director of graduate support who drew no salary whatsoever and other schools have hired experienced retired teachers as tutors and as consultants, some of whom have donated their services. Some board members also volunteer considerable time to development and other activities in support of the schools.

The extent to which the schools make available the services of social workers, counselors, and reading specialists to students contributes to costs, as does the extent to which schools provide special educational services to students and mentoring or consulting services to their teachers. Additional expenses are incurred as well when a school seeks to employ a librarian, custodian, or office assistant. Some schools have no one on staff in these positions and a few have some of these services supplied by a neighboring church.

Special Programs

How a school administers its graduate support program also affects operating costs. In some schools, the graduate support program director serves full time in that capacity, although in most schools this person also has part-time teaching responsibilities. In addition, some of the Nativity schools provide partial scholarship funding for its graduates who attend private and parochial high schools while others help families secure funding from the high schools themselves.

Costs to operate the summer programs also vary considerably. These programs, which can cost upwards of $1,000 to $1,500 per child, are sometimes a focus for budget cuts as well. For example, one school that was experiencing significant budget challenges was planning to redesign its summer program by operating it as a day program at the school rather than as a sleepaway camp in order to cut costs. A similar situation was presented at one other school in the study as well. Other schools provide very rich summer programs with large staffs that take the students off campus to retreat complexes or camps that involve considerable expense, even if the space is donated and the government subsidizes some of the meals.

Another program feature that affects costs is the extent of the sports programs offered. Some schools simply cannot afford the transportation and operating costs of sports teams, as very few schools have a gymnasium within their school building or adequate outdoor field space at or near the school. Similarly, a school's ability to support short and long-distance field trips is affected by transportation costs. At the time of my visits, several schools were facing the difficulty presented by insurance companies' refusals to underwrite policies to insure fifteen-passenger vans that had been used to transport students for athletic events and field trips because they had been deemed unsafe.

The school with the largest cost per student, a coeducational school in Boston, incurs costs not faced by other Nativity schools because of the number of services it has committed to its students as a result of the lack of access to proper health care and psychological services for the families of many of its students. This situation affects this school more than others because it selects students largely by lottery (among applicants who qualify financially) and admits a substantial number of students from the foster-care system who often have significant medical and mental health needs. This school also has the additional expense of paying off a relatively new school building.

New Schools

Considerable expense is incurred to conduct a feasibility study to determine whether the demand exists in a community to support a new Nativity school and to begin the process of planning for a new school. The Cassin Educational Initiative Foundation in Massachusetts has contributed considerable resources to feasibility studies and other programs involving Nativity and San Miguel schools and the NativityMiguel Network provides information to groups interested in conducting feasibility studies for new schools. The network also helps with school planning by providing sample feasibility studies, bylaws, handbooks for teachers, parents, and students, teacher and administrator job descriptions, and admissions application forms, in addition to curriculum guidelines. These documents help planners for new schools anticipate the tasks to be addressed and expenses to be met.

PER PUPIL COST COMPARISONS

The per pupil cost of educating a Nativity school student is clearly more than that for public schools, as figures from the U. S. Census Bureau (2006) show. States or municipalities recording the highest costs per student for the 2003–2004 school year include New York State, the District of Columbia, and Massachusetts, with per pupil costs of $12,930, $12,801 and $10,693, respectively. The Massachusetts Department of Education (2006) reported that the per pupil expenditures for Boston public schools was $12,872. The average per-pupil expenditure for the country as a whole in 2003–2004 was approximately $8,300 and the average in Maryland where two of the Nativity schools in the study are located was $9,212 per student.

In his recent book, Jonathan Kozol (2005) broke down some of these figures further and showed how wealthier suburban school districts spend considerably more per pupil than do urban districts. For example, he reported that Manhasset public schools, where only 5 percent of its students are considered low income, spent over $22,000 per pupil in 2002–2003, nearly twice as much as was spent by New York City schools.

Per pupil costs in nonsectarian and parochial schools are comparable to those reported by the Nativity schools. For example, the tuition at one Baltimore area parochial school attended by several Nativity graduates is listed as

$12,260, a figure that reportedly covers about 86 percent of the cost of educating each student (making the per pupil cost approximately $14,300). Tuitions at other independent private schools are typically much higher than parochial school tuitions (NCES, 2004c). These cost comparisons suggest that Nativity school students are receiving the kind of education more typically afforded children from more economically advantaged families who can pay the private and parochial school tuitions. They also illustrate the shameful state of public education in the United States that continues to discriminate against urban children and contributes to the need for more schools like those in the NativityMiguel network.

OVERSIGHT

A board of trustees, or directors, which can range in size from a dozen to over two dozen individuals, oversees the operations of each Nativity school. A school's board is usually composed of members of the religious order or orders that founded and operate the school as well as members of the financial, legal, and educational professions from the greater community. In some cases, a school will have both a board of trustees and a corporate board that includes only members of the religious community or communities that founded and continue to sponsor and support the school. The corporate board serves as the ultimate authority on major decisions of the board of directors and ensures that the school is governed according to the mission of the religious order or orders. The foundation board in St. Petersburg, Florida, a group of community leaders without ties to any religious entity, oversees the operation of two schools currently in operation and the future opening of two more schools in the area. As expected, the schools' boards are composed of some of the city's movers and shakers with strong contacts among the powerful and financially wealthy members of the community, as well as some experienced and influential educators and members of nonprofit agencies.

I was able to interview the board president and attend a board meeting at one of the Boston schools during my visit. The president initially became involved in the school as a volunteer tutor who, along with a friend, led a very successful capital campaign that enabled the school to purchase and renovate an old government building in Dorchester that had been gathering dust for a number of years. No longer a tutor at the school, she spent a great deal of time with fund-raising and other board activities. The thirty members of the board that she leads are very active with committee work, meetings, and fund-raising activities and seem to be as excited about the school as she is. Each member sits on one of the committees that address issues related to development, facilities management, diversity, finance, education, and human resources and compensation. Twenty-four board members attended the meeting at which I was present.

DEVELOPMENT APPROACHES AND ACTIVITIES

Boards of trustees at the Nativity schools are, naturally, very involved in monitoring the budgets of the schools as well as contributing to fund-raising activities. In soliciting contributions from private donors, board members and presidents actively seek to interest community members in the mission and activities of the schools through invitations for school visits, cocktail parties (often held at the school), and other meetings at which potential donors can meet and hear testimonies from students and teachers at the schools.

Development operations at Nativity schools range from one individual to an office staff of four, depending on the needs and fund-raising objectives of the schools. The Boston coeducational school with the highest cost per student has a fairly sophisticated approach to donor grooming and raising funds to meet the high annual operating expenses and the debt service on their relatively new building. To meet their considerable financial need, the school was operating both a capital campaign and annual giving campaign at the time of my visit and employed two professional staff members to do so. In its attempt to continually increase its donor base, the school sends out two mass mailings a year, one of which contains the school's annual report and the other a major solicitation. Members of the board host a number of cocktail and dinner parties throughout the year to expose new people to the mission of the school, which are then followed up with personal invitations to visit the school. A large gala is a major event that is held in May for which nearly 300 tickets at $250 per person are sold. As with other Nativity schools, grant funding is solicited as well for qualifying programs.

Another large fund-raising effort is conducted by a private foundation that is responsible for the founding and operation of the St. Petersburg school and a second newer school in Tampa. The foundation was formed by corporate leaders and educators who had met Fr. Jack Podsiadlo and visited Nativity Mission School where he was located before becoming director of the Nativity network. Impressed with the model and committed to providing a quality education in the St. Petersburg-Tampa area for children of color placed at risk, the founders provided some of their own funds and raised contributions from private individuals and corporations with the goal of eventually opening four schools in the area. The foundation is operated by a board of five and employs an executive director in addition to a director and a vice president of development.

One of the primary fund-raising strategies used by the foundation is to secure sponsorships of one or more students in a class of fifteen students at $12,000 per student. Corporations are solicited strongly as they can earn tax credits equal to 50 percent of the amount of a donation that supports the education of a child from a low-income family. The foundation has been fortunate to have raised funds to provide a small endowment for the school. (Most Nativity schools lack an endowment.) It has also secured funding and community exposure through a significant professional golf tour event in the area at which the students and staff volunteer and from which the school receives proceeds.

Seeking sponsors for the majority of the cost of providing the education for a student is a common approach among Nativity schools, although the scholarship amount sought varies from school to school. In some cases, sponsors are asked to commit to the scholarship amount for the three or four years during which the student will attend the school. In some schools, students maintain some contact with their sponsors through mail correspondence; in other schools, student scholarship recipients are not identified to the sponsors.

Two schools in the study had very modest development programs and faced financial struggles as a result. At both of these schools, most of the development activity was handled by one individual who was not an experienced fund-raiser, although school administrators provided some direction and initiated contacts with potential donors. Members of the boards were also active in promoting the school and identifying sources of funding. The primary activity of the development officer, then, was to plan and produce mailings that included an annual report and a direct appeal. Most of the schools produced an annual report that helped them generate interest by promoting the accomplishments of the school and their students and identifying school needs.

Formal and informal partnerships with businesses, corporations, and other institutions have supplied the schools with much needed resources and helped the schools expand the services that could be offered to the students and their families. Perhaps the most significant partnership involving a Nativity school has been THEARC community in Washington, DC, which opened in the fall of 2005 and involves the Washington Middle School for Girls among its nine partners. Funded by a nonprofit organization formed by a local corporation, THEARC is part of a revitalization of an area in the 8th Ward referred to as "East of the River." Informal partnerships exist as well, such as one I became aware of recently through a student of mine whose father provides optical services free of charge to students at one of the Nativity schools. I also had a conversation recently with a business executive in Delaware with a strong interest in improving educational opportunities for children from low-income homes with a better education and who, along with his wife, has been a strong supporter of a relatively new Nativity school for boys in his area. He has carried his passion further to help the Nativity school add a fifth grade and fund a summer camp program for incoming students to the school, in addition to leading plans to open a Nativity school for girls and getting more members of the business community involved in his endeavors. As several of the Nativity administrators reported to me, when people hear about the great things the Nativity schools are doing for urban children placed at risk, their hearts and checkbooks open up.

The Nativity Educational Centers Network, now the NativityMiguel Network of Schools, is set up to help new schools come to fruition and support existing schools through national fund-raising efforts and national meetings to share best practices in fund raising, administration, graduate support, curriculum development, and effective instruction. By combining the two very similar models of middle school education with a consistent mission and set of goals, the new network feels it has the potential to secure large sources of funding that can benefit all of the network schools and raise awareness on a large scale about the value of these schools.

EIGHT

Summary of Findings,
Conclusions, and Implications

THE ORIGINAL NATIVITY middle school program came to fruition from both careful planning and serendipity, and possibly a certain amount of prayer, but with the clear purpose of providing boys from the lower east side of Manhattan with the academic skills needed to earn admission into and succeed in selective parochial high schools and later in college. This small independent enterprise has grown into a significant social justice ministry to underserved urban children and their families. Today, on its Web site, the NativityMiguel Network of Schools boasts of the existence of sixty-four schools with over 4,300 enrolled students and more than 2,000 graduates.

I conducted this study to examine just how the Nativity model was being implemented more than thirty-five years after the first Nativity school was founded, to document the levels of academic success and educational attainment of Nativity students, and to examine factors that have contributed to the success of the students and the schools. I also set out to describe and examine aspects of the Nativity schools that contribute to students' social, emotional, spiritual, and physical development during the crucial middle school years. In this effort, I collected standardized test score, attendance, and report card data, administered surveys to students and teachers, and visited eleven Nativity schools where I conducted school and classroom visits and interviews with various stakeholders.

ACADEMIC SUCCESS

Evidence that the Nativity model schools have been effective in accelerating the academic progress of urban children placed at risk is strong. My findings show that students' academic gains during their middle school years significantly and substantially exceeded those of children from similar backgrounds attending urban parochial and public schools. In most cases, standardized test score gains of Nativity students exceeded the equivalent of one grade level per year. Findings from this study are consistent with one that documented the levels of academic success and educational attainment of students at the original Nativity Mission Center school a few years ago. These findings, published in the *Journal of Education for Students Placed At Risk* (Podsiadlo & Philliber, 2003), showed how the levels of academic achievement and educational attainment of Nativity Mission's students (most of whom were of Puerto Rican or Dominican heritage) substantially exceeded those of Hispanic boys across the country. In small but powerful ways, Nativity schools are contributing to the narrowing of what is known as the racial achievement gap.

Results of this study show that Nativity schools provide children placed at risk with an environment that represents the best practices of effective urban middle schools. Among these practices are the small school size and small classes for instruction that enable teachers to monitor closely the academic progress of each student and devise approaches to meet individual academic needs. The small size of the schools, the largest of which educates ninety-six boys and girls in grades five through eight, also enables principals and faculty advisors to get to know well each student and the student's family. It also enables teachers and administrators to keep a careful eye on each student and attend to each one's academic and social struggles. In no other school program where "individual attention" to students is promoted have I witnessed what is truly individual attention. Nativity schools commit themselves to every one of their students and work hard to help each student succeed. There is very little attrition in Nativity schools.

Certainly, however, Nativity schools are not the only ones in which urban children placed at risk succeed. Other larger urban middle school endeavors, such as KIPP (Knowledge Is Power Program) schools, have documented high levels of student academic success as well (KIPP Foundation, 2007). Important aspects of their programs that contribute to their success are an extended day, the availability of teachers at home in the evening by phone, and well-trained and committed principals. KIPP students and their parents must also sign a pledge to abide by school rules and commit themselves to the level of academic work required. But theses schools cannot provide the level of individual care and guidance where needed that the Nativity schools can, and concerns have been raised about high attrition rates at KIPP schools (Robelen, 2007).

IMPLICATIONS OF THE ADMISSIONS PROCESS

Children and parents are made aware during the admissions process that the academic expectations and demands of a Nativity education are high and necessary if the students are to overcome the deficits from their elementary school education. The admissions process, which involves interviews with and written essays from parents and children and observations of the student applicants in academic and social settings during the spring or summer prior to matriculation, enables school personnel to evaluate the commitment and fit of the students to the school program. Through this process, school personnel are better able to determine whether a child can function cooperatively in a group setting and engage in the learning process. In this way, it helps the schools to screen for behavioral and emotional problems, as well as for severe learning difficulties, that the schools lack the resources to address adequately. Once a Nativity school opens its doors and children begin to demonstrate academic success, other parents quickly take notice and seek admission for their children as well.

Some critics of the Nativity school model cite the admissions process as evidence that the students experience the academic success they do because they are handpicked. Clearly, some selection takes place and the very fact that parents or guardians have to take certain steps in order to have their children considered for admission demonstrates that they possess at least some level of commitment to providing their children with a good education. However, results of this study also offer evidence that screening students for admission is not always necessary for students to experience high levels of academic success. For example, the school that selects its students by lottery and purposely admits one-fourth of its students from the foster-care system has one of the best records for academic gains among the Nativity schools in the study, with 79 percent of its students gaining one grade equivalent or more per year in standardized reading achievement tests and 66 percent with similar gains in mathematics. To accomplish this level of success, this school also has one of the lowest student–teacher ratios among Nativity schools at 4.4 students per teacher and the largest per pupil expenditure because of the level of services it must provide its students. Critics should acknowledge also that most of the Nativity schools' recruiting efforts are directed specifically to poor-performing, high-poverty local public elementary schools. Nativity school personnel are wise to use the criteria that they do so as not to admit students with significant behavioral or learning difficulties or without a desire to succeed, characteristics that could undermine the quality of learning for other students, especially considering that the Nativity schools, except for one, lack the financial resources to remediate significant difficulties. As research (Brody et al., 2003) has shown, the behaviors and attitudes of minority children from high-poverty neighborhoods are influenced by a multitude of adverse factors that may render severe conduct problems difficult to modify. Unfortunately, not every child will be able to thrive in a Nativity school.

Regardless of the schools' admissions processes, parents and guardians must meet certain income restrictions before their children are even considered for admission. In this study, a higher percentage of the Nativity school students qualified for the federal free and reduced meal program than did students in the two urban parochial schools and six urban public middle schools in Baltimore with whom I compared Nativity students' standardized test performances. By setting an income ceiling for admission and selecting students whose test scores are below grade level, the Nativity schools ensure that they are educating children who are among those who had been "left behind" in the urban public schools. Also, by insisting that parents show some level of commitment to their children's education and development, the schools demonstrate that they recognize that incorporating a sense of community through the school serves the best interests of the students.

BETWEEN-SCHOOL DIFFERENCES

This study also showed, however, that not all Nativity schools are equally effective in accelerating students' academic skills and performances. In two schools included in this study, students' test score gains lagged behind the levels at the other Nativity schools, with less than 50 percent of students at these schools performing at or above grade level in reading or math by seventh grade. These differences in student achievement provided an opportunity to examine more closely school characteristics that could distinguish higher performing and lower performing schools that follow the same basic model of education. An examination of the school characteristics showed no evidence that school and class sizes, student–teacher ratios, or the length of the school day were factors that distinguished these two schools from the others.

However, my assessment of these schools, which were the two youngest schools I visited, suggests that at the time of the study both were still in a state of development and transition in which they were continuing to identify the right mix of students who would bring enough social and emotional strength to the demanding academic program and long school day. Testimonies from administrators as to the challenges of mastering the process of selecting students who can persist in their studies until 4 or 5 P.M. and who receive adequate support from their homes show that it takes nearly all schools several years before they are able to select students successfully. Administrators at these two schools reported more student conflict and greater struggles to get parents involved than did leaders at the other Nativity schools. Clearly there is an art to the process of identifying urban students at risk who can thrive in a demanding educational program. I also saw that these two schools were in the process of making adjustments with respect to their physical plant or administrative team that were likely to provide the structures needed to ensure greater student academic gains in the near future. In fact, at one school that had made recent significant administrative changes, standardized test score data were collected during the year in which these changes were taking place.

Several pieces of evidence collected during the course of this study suggest that a significant contributor to between-school differences in students' academic gains was the condition of the curriculum. At both of the lower performing schools, administrators acknowledged that considerable curriculum improvement efforts were under way at the time of my visit. Some of my class observations and discussions with teachers at these schools also suggested that a strengthening of the curriculum was in order. Providing a strong curriculum was an area in which some of the older Nativity schools struggled during their early years until they were able to hire administrators who had the knowledge and experience to oversee efforts to do so. Even among Nativity schools that were in operation for ten years or more, principals recognized the need to continue to strengthen and update at least some aspects of their curriculum. At the time of the study, a few schools had recently hired administrators who had strong backgrounds in curriculum development.

TEACHERS AND ADMINISTRATORS

From the results of this study, and consistent with research on successful urban schools (Trimble, 2004), I am convinced that qualities of the administrators and teachers who work with the urban children in Nativity schools make a substantial difference. They exert a strong influence on the nature of the academic and social environment and, therefore, how well or poorly students respond to the demands of a long school day. Having some teachers and at least one administrator with cultural backgrounds similar to those of the students at the school is one factor that can contribute appreciably to students' sense of belonging. In this study, I found that such a factor was valuable in terms of the role models these teachers can provide. School administrators work hard to recruit faculty from diverse backgrounds with mixed success but recognize the importance of taking these steps.

Even more important, I learned, was for teachers and administrators to possess the sensitivity to and understanding of the kinds of family and neighborhood struggles their students face, as well as the belief that their students can and will be successful. School personnel must also be able to show their students and the students' families respect and care even as they must communicate high expectations and demand quality work. As Delpit (2006b) has stated, teachers of children of color placed at risk must be authoritative, that is possessing the personal power to show that they are in control and exhibiting respect, care, and an engaging interactional style, while pushing students to set and meet high standards. Hiring faculty, whether certified or volunteer, with these characteristics is an ongoing challenge for Nativity administrators, one that they must face yearly with the high turnover of volunteer teachers.

As the results of this study suggest, experience and training are necessary for teachers to be effective, as are the authoritative characteristics described by Delpit. Teachers must have a toolbox of effective techniques at their disposal to effect substantive learning and manage student behavior. The use of a combination of skillful experienced and certified teachers and authoritative but inexperienced volunteers works well for the Nativity schools. Having years of study in a teacher certification program does not ensure that a teacher will be the kind of authoritative, caring, committed, and flexible instructor that enables urban students to flourish whether in a Nativity or any other urban school. The findings of the study show that students in schools with a rather large percentage of the teaching staff composed of volunteers can and do experience a high level of academic achievement. Two very successful schools in this study maintained a volunteer staff that amounted to approximately 70 percent of their faculties.

Findings suggest that the ways in which Nativity schools make use of their volunteer teachers are crucial. First, volunteer teachers must teach only content with which they are familiar, that is, related to the field in which they majored in college. Second, they need to have regular and expert mentoring and supervision in order to master quickly a set of techniques that enable them to plan and deliver effective lessons and manage student behavior. Third, volunteer teachers should be given responsibility for teaching classes on their own only when they have become reasonably comfortable with the children and the curriculum and their teaching load should start small and increase as they gain experience. In addition, school administrators who make effective use of the volunteer teachers for small-group or individual tutoring or instruction, as well as in team-teaching arrangements, are able to maximize the potential value of the volunteers for accelerating student achievement.

Without a doubt, the success of the Nativity school programs rests on the quality of the instruction and academic assistance students receive throughout the long school day. Competent adults must be available to supervise student athletics and other activities, spend time with them in conversation, tutor them as they struggle to learn, and help them with homework assignments, as well as facilitate their learning in regular classroom settings. Staffing a school exclusively with a full-time teaching staff that works a full 7:30 A.M. to 3:30 P.M. day, 180 to 190 days a year, will not be enough to help children who had been left behind in elementary school to develop the academic skills necessary to be competitive in the pursuit of higher education or in the increasingly complex world of work. Volunteer teachers who are willing to put in long hours with very little pay are an essential ingredient of the Nativity model because of the poor academic skill levels the children arrive with. As some of the Nativity schools move toward hiring more certified teachers and fewer volunteer teachers, the administrators also recognize the need to have a strong staff of competent volunteer tutors and homework helpers to provide learning support during the school day and extended study time. The students require long hours of instruction and support to enable them to overcome academic deficits and administrators cannot expect teachers to work sixty to eighty hours each week for too many years.

Perhaps the most essential ingredient of a successful urban middle school is a committed and talented administrative team headed by a president or principal who can lead that team with competence and sensitivity. During my school visits, I observed and interacted with such teams. One that stands out is the team at Milwaukee Jesuit Middle School, whose president and graduate support program director I have already identified. A third important member of the team is a Mexican American woman who grew up in the same community as the students. Having been appointed principal after serving for six years as the business manager and special assistant to the president, she understands her students' family and community issues well and serves as the primary contact person between home and school. The director of development, whose enthusiasm for the school was evident from the moment he picked me up at the airport, is the son of the GSP director and a product of Milwaukee Catholic schools. The involvement that these four leaders have in the Milwaukee community, their unselfish commitment to the children and their families and to social justice, and their expertise and teamwork account for a great deal of the success their students experience.

The level of commitment that Nativity teachers and administrators must take on is extraordinary; it is also physically and emotionally exhausting. Having once wondered if I could assume a teaching or administrative role in a Nativity school after my time comes to retire from the already demanding life of a college academic, I realized in conducting this study that I would not have the stamina. But this is the level of commitment that is needed to help children who have been left behind gain competence and confidence. Teaching children who have grown up in the midst of urban dysfunction is very difficult; there is no room for teachers or administrators who are biding their time until retirement or have lost the zeal for teaching. If urban children could count on having principals who were as skillful, committed, and caring as many of the Nativity school leaders, they would succeed at rates greater than they do at present.

PARENTS, GRADUATE SUPPORT, AND HOLISTIC EDUCATION

Nativity schools are able to accomplish more than other school programs because of three factors that are unique to the small Nativity schools by which strong school communities are established that involve parents intimately and ensure that students continue to succeed in challenging high school programs. First, by engaging the parents in the school program through school meetings, celebrations, and outings, the admissions process that includes open houses, and parent service to the school, Nativity schools take away the concern that most urban parents with little education have about approaching school personnel. Most Nativity schools are quite effective at demonstrating to parents that their participation and support are vital to their child's school success. As research (Borman, Benson, & Overman, 2005) has shown, taking steps to involve parents in the school community in meaningful ways provides parents with the social capital that strengthens their connection to the school and tends to commit them more to supporting their children's academic engagement and social development. If the schools were much larger, the administrators and teachers would not be able to work so closely with the students and their families.

A second factor unique to the schools, the graduate support program, is a component of all Nativity schools whereby resources are directed to ensure that middle school graduates receive the continued support needed to address academic and personal challenges that arise and continue to flourish in high school and beyond. Experience has shown that, even with the strong academic background that the middle school component of the Nativity program provides, many students continue to face difficult challenges and destructive neighborhood influences that can undermine continued academic success. It is not unusual for graduate support program directors to offer personal counseling and support to a number of graduates. Continued contact with Nativity graduates also helps keep them focused on college attendance and career success. No other school initiative to date has provided this kind of ongoing support for urban students placed at risk.

The third factor that sets Nativity schools apart from other successful urban middle school programs and which requires the small school size characteristic of the schools is their commitment to educating the whole person of strong character for leadership and service. Leadership development and caring for one another are important aspects of summer camps and other school programs. School personnel work with students to help them learn effective interpersonal conflict resolution and problem-solving skills through the summer camps and various school-year activities, including prayer and reflection services, community service, spiritual retreats, small group advisories, individual and group counseling, and classes that address moral issues that young adolescents face. Nativity administrators have pointed out that increasing enrollments would compromise these aspects of the students' education.

Underlying these three factors is the central quality of relationship. Nativity schools are places where faculty, staff, and administration go out of their way to support students in their development and help them discover their unique gifts. Students learn early on that they are respected and cared for and come to understand that school personnel are interested in helping and supporting them for years after they leave middle school.

The strong mission to educate for social change that underlies the Nativity school philosophy leads the schools to provide more than a strong academic program and continued academic support in high school. By participating in the Nativity educational program, young people learn that the hope for all graduates is that they will use the education they receive for social change by exemplifying strong moral character and being a model of right living, leadership, and service to family and community. Nativity schools help students gain social and economic capital through an education that helps build academic and leadership skills and engages the students in meaningful service and reflection and also encourages continued leadership and service. This is the path by which Nativity schools seek to reduce economic poverty, human hopelessness, and urban decay.

EXEMPLARY GRADUATES

Many Nativity school graduates have demonstrated these qualities during and beyond their high school and college years. The NativityMiguel Network of Schools (n.d.) Web site provides profiles of three such graduates. One of the featured individuals, José de Jesus Peralta, a 1987 graduate of Nativity Mission Center, is serving as a senior guidance counselor at the Catholic high school in New York City that he attended. In his testimony, José cited his experiences at the school, and summer camp in particular, as important influences in his development that helped remove the harsh exterior of a New York street kid and direct him and his schoolmates along a path to a productive and exemplary life of service.

Similar sentiments were expressed by the three Nativity Mission alumni who were on staff at their alma mater at the time of my visits. These three men demonstrated an incredibly strong commitment to the Nativity approach of educating and expressed strong desires to give back by committing their professional lives to working with the new generation of students from some of the same neighborhoods where they grew up. In addition to being valuable models and teachers for their students, they were also modeling right living in the community. One of the men, the graduate support program director, was also a valuable resource for the students' families as he was often called upon to help some families with their struggles and conflicts.

During the summer of 2007, I interviewed two African American men who graduated from two different Baltimore Nativity schools. Turned down by the all-boys school because of his self-acknowledged behavioral problems, Ricardo obtained admission to the co-institutional Nativity school for seventh grade. Growing up in a female-headed household, he was in dire need of male mentoring and a school that would insist on proper behavior and help him develop effective social skills. His mentors came in the form of a religious brother who taught at the school and two members of the school's board. Among the valuable lessons he learned from his Nativity education were the importance of a firm handshake and looking someone in the eye. He developed a sense of gratitude for what he received that he sees giving back as a nonnegotiable part of who he is. After a successful high school experience, he emerged as a strong servant leader in college who led fundraising efforts and served in such leadership positions as student government president. As he prepared to attend law school, he looked ahead to how he wants to serve as a mentor for others and address ways in which he could contribute to a more just society in which many more people could participate meaningfully.

The second Baltimore Nativity graduate I interviewed also followed a path of exemplary leadership and service through high school and college. Dennis graduated from a Jesuit college three years earlier, after serving as a resident advisor, an officer in the Black Student Association, and an academic mentor. At the time I met with him, he had completed a second master's degree, was working for a nonprofit law center where he was supervising employees who made referrals to citizens seeking legal services, and was contemplating going to law school. He demonstrated a sincere interest in political issues and expressed a desire to continue to work to find ways of helping people who are not being served well by the government.

Of course, not all Nativity graduates achieve this level of academic and professional success or demonstrate the quality of leadership and commitment to improving the welfare of those who are disadvantaged. Some graduates, despite considerable effort on the part of Nativity school teachers and administrators, struggle to complete high school and get bogged down in the dysfunction of family or neighborhood. However, as one of my interviewees indicated, had it not been for the education and mentoring provided by his Nativity school he doubts that he would have ever attended college. Although the long hours, extended days, and summer programs keep Nativity students away from dysfunctional influences, Nativity schools do not exert the only influence on their students' lives.

The stories these graduates shared with me also underscore a primary principle taught by one of my graduate school professors that an individual's development is a product of the interaction of one's environmental influences and one's own personal qualities. Jose's, Ricardo's, and Dennis's successes came about because of their own personal qualities that enabled them to respond well to a Nativity education. The important point, however, is that without the environment provided by Nativity schools, as well as by their high schools and colleges, their personal qualities were not likely to have led them to the levels of success and leadership they have achieved.

A CRITIQUE OF THE STUDY

As with any study that seeks to evaluate the success of an educational endeavor, the one presented here, even with its use of multiple methods of data collection, has its share of limitations. First and foremost among those limitations is the level of bias brought to the study by its principal and, for the most part, sole investigator. As objective as I have tried to be, aware of the importance of objectivity in program evaluation and research, I have been sold on the value of the Nativity schools as I have observed two of Baltimore's Nativity schools grow into wonderful academies of learning and positive young adolescent development since they opened in 1993. However, as much as I would have liked to find that all the Nativity schools were able to report outstanding academic success, such was not the case, as I have shown.

Because of the small number of schools involved in the study, the even smaller number for which complete data were collected, and the lack of random selection of schools for the study, the selected schools may not represent well the entire network of Nativity schools. In addition, this study was limited to those schools that had been in existence for at least several years and had the benefit of experience to improve their programs. At the same time, there was variation in school size, location, per pupil expenditures, grade-level and gender configurations, and commitment to utilizing volunteer teachers, as well variation in student racial and cultural characteristics, that informed the selection of schools for the study. Suffice it to say that this study provides a snapshot of some of the more established Nativity schools, although their levels of academic success were not considered in the selection process. All schools contacted for inclusion in the study agreed to participate and allow me to visit, but a few felt they could not commit the classroom time to administer student surveys or the administrative time to supply student academic data, time-consuming tasks indeed. In return for opening their doors to me, I sent all schools, including the comparison schools, a brief report of the findings of the study, including a summary of the data collected for each school along with the set of Nativity schools and comparison schools.

I must recognize, too, as I have mentioned in chapter 4, that caution needs to be exercised with respect to drawing cause-and-effect inferences from the test score, report card grade, and survey data presented here, as survey data represent student and teacher perceptions at a point in time that does not coincide with or precede students' academic performances. What does contribute to the confidence I have with respect to some of the inferences made is the availability of multiple sources of data in the surveys, school report cards, standardized test scores, observations, and interviews that lead to consistent conclusions.

IMPLICATIONS

At the very least, findings from this study of eleven Nativity schools offer further confirmation of the conclusions drawn from the results of many other research studies about effective middle school education for urban children placed at risk. In an environment that screams for models of effective urban middle school education, the education provided by Nativity schools shines more light on the factors that make a difference. With standardized test scores among urban middle school students deplorably low and not getting any better, alternative models of middle school education are sorely needed.

Urban educators, board members, politicians, and funding organizations would be wise to recognize that urban children are served best in educational environments that are reasonable in size and staffed by principals, assistant principals, teachers, aides, and guidance counselors who can function effectively as a team and who hold high expectations of one another and of their students. In addition, the curriculum must be based on appropriate standards and characterized by increasing complexity and challenge, as instructional leaders in Nativity schools have recognized. As Nativity school leaders have done, other school officials should be sure to continue to evaluate their curricula and ensure that a well-educated and experienced academic leader directs the curriculum reviews. More partnerships, like the one among the three Boston schools I visited had with respect to their shared science curriculum, should be explored and funded.

Structures are important, and the Nativity structural elements that call for an extended day, small class sizes and advisories, and rich summer programs are essential components of the model that, if implemented in more urban schools, could lead to impressive academic and social gains for many more children. For example, summer programs that engage students in learning activities are critical for urban children placed at risk because of the negative effects that summer breaks have on the academic skills of children from low income environments (Cooper, Nye, Charlton, Lindsay, & Greathouse, 1996). However, structures and high expectations alone will not help bring about substantial change without the involvement of committed, competent, and caring educators who teach a curriculum that challenges the students. I believe that one of the greatest challenges facing the education enterprise today is its failure to attract these people into the high-poverty schools. An important lesson from the success of Nativity schools is that "if you build it, they will come." That is, if schools are organized well with competent and inspired leaders, competent and inspired teachers will follow. The evidence for this contention is found in the Nativity schools that have no trouble attracting these people and Teach for America that continues to grow and attract talented people. In fact, both programs turn down many applicants. The KIPP school movement is further evidence that the principal and teachers make a difference, as my visit to Baltimore's KIPP Ujima Village Academy showed. This also is one of the lessons that the Talent Development Middle Schools efforts have provided (Balfanz & Mac Iver, 2000). Of course, the urban middle school leaders must also maintain their commitments to forming effective learning communities in order to keep competent teachers.

Results of this study show how important establishing a social and learning climate that focuses on building mutually respectful relationships is to school effectiveness and student engagement and achievement. As I demonstrated in chapter 4, students who perceived their school environment as enjoyable with rules that were fair, their academic classes as more engaging and learning-focused, and the peer social climate of the schools to be more friendly tended to be more motivated to persist in their school work and perform better academically even when the work was difficult. Interviews with students also showed that they will engage in learning when the climate of the school and classrooms is supportive and respectful, the responsibility for which lies squarely on the shoulders of the teachers and administrators.

Many of the Nativity schools personnel, including board members, have engaged in discussions of whether to expand the size of their schools by admitting more students into the existing classes. However, rather than increasing the size of the classes, some school leaders, seeing the poor academic skills that so many of their students bring to middle school, have given strong consideration to expanding the number of grades by adding a fifth or fourth grade to the program if more classrooms were available. Recently, one of the Nativity schools was able to acquire a second campus location that enabled it to add a fourth grade.

Certainly, Nativity (or NativityMiguel) schools cannot meet the needs of all urban children placed at risk. There are simply too many children in need of a better education in the cities. Urban school districts must pay attention to what the practices of NativityMiguel, KIPP, and Talent Development schools offer. I am saddened to see that urban school districts are moving in directions inconsistent with what the research on these educational models shows. In Baltimore, for example, the city school board has closed schools in order to use building space more efficiently—that is, to put as many children as it can in the fewest number of school buildings. Such an approach fails to recognize the value of smaller, community-oriented middle schools and makes whole-school reform more difficult to achieve. The urban public middle schools are simply too large to be able to provide the level of services that their students require in order to acquire the academic skills needed to succeed in today's heavily technological global economy. Smaller urban middle schools that educate urban children placed at risk do cost more per pupil than larger ones, but the success of the Nativity schools shows that the extra funding pays off. The work that is under way to improve public high schools across the nation that the Bill and Melinda Gates Foundation has prompted and sponsored must be directed toward our middle schools as well.

Fortunately, the Nativity model is being applied to some larger schools that educate children in elementary as well as middle school. For example, the Gesu School in Philadelphia is a PreK–8 parochial school in a high-poverty area of North Philadelphia that has adopted aspects of the Nativity model that include an administrative team structure of president, principal, and development director, and elements such as summer enrichment programs, afternoon homework assistance, and low tuition. The school emphasizes academic achievement, along with leadership and character development, and focuses on preparing all students for successful high school experiences. It has no particular requirements for admission, although the school recruits children from low-income homes.

CLOSING REFLECTIONS

As I bring this book to a close, I call to mind various images from my travels and interactions. Among these is the memory of my meeting with a room full of Mexican immigrant parents at the Milwaukee school. With extraordinary gratitude and limited English proficiency, they applauded the president, a Jesuit priest, and the graduate support program director for all that they, two white men, had given their sons. Their testimonies showed the value of a strong community with the school at the center.

I recall, too, the stories that some of the Nativity teachers told about how they came to become involved in their school. Several full-time, certified teachers had first entered the schools as volunteer teachers unsure of whether they wanted to pursue a career in teaching, much less teaching in an urban school. A woman who was serving as an administrator and teacher at one of the schools for girls had first taught at another Nativity school. Learning about the former Nativity teachers who went on to head or help establish newer Nativity schools showed me how committed many Nativity people are to spreading the model and helping more children access a high-quality education.

The inspired and inspiring work of Nativity teachers and administrators provides a message of hope, a hope for a better tomorrow that forms the foundation of the teachings of many religious and spiritual traditions. Being an educator is to live the message of hope for the students' tomorrows and the tomorrow of a more just and inclusive society. Also, being an educator is to act out of love—love for children and love for the work of helping to transform society, a few children at a time.

The creation of the first Nativity middle schools marked the beginning of an educational venture that was new to the Jesuits who have operated dozens of colleges and universities, as well as high schools, for centuries. The Nativity school movement has been a natural extension of the social justice mission of the Jesuit and other religious orders that is an essential expression of the faith their communities hold dear. As important and valuable as these religious traditions are, leaders of Nativity schools without such foundations have shown that they can also meet the spiritual, in addition to the academic and social, needs of their students. I look forward to seeing more private individuals and groups pursue the founding of schools that can become a part of the NativityMiguel Network or to pursue supporting new and struggling existing schools by incorporating aspects of the Nativity model that can accelerate student academic achievement as well as leadership and character development.

The formation of the Nativity Educational Centers Network in 2001, and more recently the establishment of the NativityMiguel Network of Schools in 2006 from a merger of the Nativity and Miguel networks, is helping to make NativityMiguel schools stronger. The network provides a mechanism for communication among schools by sponsoring national meetings for principals, graduate support directors, teachers, and development officers. At these meetings, workshops are presented where best practices are shared and personnel of newer schools can learn from the experiences of their counterparts in more established schools. The programs sponsored by the network will continue to be a valuable asset to new schools, as well as those in the planning stages.

Educators responsible for policy decisions at the local, state, and national levels would be wise to attend to the less-is-more wisdom of the Nativity model. This is a model that shows how programs directed at the school level and supported by an umbrella organization that provides guidance and support, rather than excessive demands for time-consuming paperwork that compromises instructional quality, can help students placed at risk exceed at outstanding levels. The creation of small independent schools may also make it easier for schools to form partnerships with the business and higher education communities that can benefit all parties. My research has shown that many individuals and businesses would be interested, if not anxious, to support and fund effective educational endeavors for children placed at risk.

With the lack of substantial improvement in urban education cited by so many educational researchers (e.g., Rist, 2000) over the past few decades and the failure of *Brown v. the Board of Education* to effect substantial change with respect to access to educational quality, new models of urban education must be considered and implemented. Because the problem of social injustice is larger than substandard urban education, Nativity schools and others like them are taking small but important steps toward effecting substantial social change. As Noguera (2005) has charged, the problems of education are only a part of the larger problem of social inequality. Too many members of the educational and political establishment lack the will, not the knowledge, to provide a high-quality education to all children.

Such is not the case among Nativity educators and supporters. They possess both the will and the knowledge.

APPENDIX A

The Schools, Their Students, and Their Teachers

In consultation with the Director of the Nativity Educational Centers Network, I initially selected twelve schools for the evaluation study. Of the thirty-nine schools listed by the Nativity Network as Nativity model schools in 2003, those schools founded in 1999 or thereafter (twenty-two schools) were eliminated from the study because they were too young to have a formal graduate support program in place. Of the remaining seventeen schools on the list, twelve were chosen initially to capture variation in school structures (grades six through eight or five through eight), student characteristics (all-boys, all-girls, or coeducational; different racial-ethnic backgrounds), and locations. Six of these twelve schools had provided standardized test score data during the spring and summer of 2002 to the Nativity Education Centers Network. One of the initial twelve schools was eliminated from the study after my visit to the school because, as a Pre-K–8 elementary school with its Nativity students representing only approximately one-third of its middle school student body, it did not adequately meet the criteria for a Nativity middle school. The eleven schools chosen for the study varied in longevity from six (three schools founded in 1997) to thirty-three years (one school founded in 1971), with five of the schools entering their eleventh year of operation. The schools selected for the present study are listed in Table A.1, along with school characteristics such as school religious affiliations, grade arrangements, numbers of students by gender, and primary racial/ethnic group served. Students were not asked to identify their religious affiliation, although Nativity school administrators indicated that the majority of Latino children were Catholic and the majority of African American children represented a number of Christian and Muslim religious groups, with very few of the students being Catholic.

TABLE A.1
Nativity Schools Included in the 2003–2004 Study

School*	City Location	Year School Opened	Religious or Other Affiliation	Grade Arrangement/ Enrollment	Primary Racial-Ethnic Group
NYCG	New York	1993	Society of the Holy Child Jesus	5–8 / 62 girls	Hispanic
NYCB	New York	1971	Society of Jesus	6–8 / 60 boys	Hispanic
BOSG	Boston	1993	School Sisters of Notre Dame	5–8 / 60 girls	Cape Verdean African American, Hispanic, Caribbean
BOSB	Boston	1990	Society of Jesus	5–8 / 66 boys	African American
BOSC	Boston	1997	Episcopal Church of Boston	5–8 / 40 boys, 41 girls	African American, Cape Verdean, Hispanic, Caribbean
WASG	Washington, DC	1997	Society of the Holy Child Jesus	5–8 / 52 girls	African American
BALB	Baltimore	1993	Society of Jesus	6–8 / 70 boys	African American
BALC	Baltimore	1993	Five Religious Communities	6–8 / 34 boys, 34 girls	African American, Hispanic, Caucasian
MILB	Milwaukee, WI	1993	Society of Jesus	6–8 / 53 boys	Hispanic (Mexican)
NORB	New Orleans	1994	Society of St. Edmund	5–8 / 60 boys	African American, Creole
STPC	St. Petersburg, FL	1997	Private Citizens	5–8 / 49 boys, 47 girls	African American

Total Student Enrollment: 432 boys (59%) and 296 girls (41%; 728 total)

Note: *School coding: The first three letters designate the city and the fourth letter designates whether the school educated boys only (B), girls only (G), or both boys and girls (C).

Four of the Nativity schools that educate boys only were founded and are operated by the Society of Jesus, or Jesuit, order of Catholic men, including the two oldest schools in the Nativity network. The fifth all-boys school is operated by another order of Catholic priests, the Society of St. Edmund, or Edmundites. Four of the Nativity schools, including the three all-girls schools, were founded and are operated by Catholic religious orders of women, with the coeducational school in Baltimore including a religious order of men among its six founding groups. The Episcopal diocese of Boston founded and operates a coeducational school and a private group of citizens from the St. Petersburg-Tampa Bay area of Florida operates the third coeducational school included in the study, one of two Nativity schools in the network without any religious affiliation. (Coeducational Nativity schools are described alternatively as *co-institutional* because most instruction takes place in single-sex classes.)

Among the eleven Nativity schools included in the study, seven had a 5–8 grade structure and the remaining four a 6–8 structure. During the 2003–2004 academic year, the four 6–8 schools enrolled a mean of nearly sixty-three students (approximately twenty-one per grade) and the seven 5–8 schools enrolled a mean of sixty-eight students (approximately seventeen per grade). (The Boston school for boys enrolls a very small fifth-grade class, about one-half the size of the sixth-grade class.) Student-teacher ratios in Nativity schools averaged 5.6 to 1, the median class size for instruction was twelve, and students attended school for a mean of nine to ten hours per day.

NATIVITY STUDENTS

Of the 516 Nativity school students who completed surveys for the present study (71 percent of the enrollment in the eleven schools and 90 percent of the 572 students enrolled in the nine schools where student surveys were administered), 49 percent self-identified as African American or black, 35 percent as Hispanic or Latino/Latina, 11 percent as biracial or multiracial (most of which included African or black designations), 2 percent as white, and 2 percent as Asian. Complete data for the analyses were available for 470 students. The mean age of the Nativity students in the study was 12.3 years (SD = 1.0) and 94 percent of the students qualified for federal free or reduced price meals.

NATIVITY TEACHERS

During the 2003–2004 school year, the eleven Nativity schools employed a total of fifty-eight volunteer teachers (mean of 5.3 per school) and the equivalent of 68.9 experienced teachers in a full-time or part-time capacity (mean of 6.3 per school; see Table A.2). In all the schools, individuals who held administrative positions also taught one or more classes. With respect to surveys administered to teachers to assess teachers' self-perceptions and perceptions of their students and school environments, 101 teachers at nine Nativity schools completed them (96 percent response rate). Forty of these respondents were first- ($N = 19$) or second-year ($N = 21$) volunteer teachers and sixty-one were full-time experienced teachers, with a mean of 15.2 years experience. The latter group was composed of teachers with a full-time, full-pay contract. (Some

TABLE A.2
Characteristics of Teaching Staffs in Nativity Schools

School	Number of Teachers in the School (FTEs)	Number of Volunteer Teachers	% of Staff Composed of Volunteer Teachers
NYC Girls	8.6	5	58
NYC Boys	9.5	5	53
Boston Girls	10	7	70
Boston Boys	15.6	11	71
Boston Coed	18	11	61
Washington, DC, Girls	7.8	1	13
Baltimore Boys	11.8	5	42
Baltimore Coed	10.5	3	29
Milwaukee Boys	11.2	3	27
New Orleans Boys	8.3	4	48
St. Petersburg, Coed	14.6	3	21
Nativity School Totals	125.9	58	46.1

of these teachers also had administrative responsibilities.) Among the volunteer teachers, sixteen (40 percent) were men and twenty-four (60 percent) were women. Seventy-five percent identified themselves as Caucasian, 15 percent as African American or black, and the remaining 10 percent in other racial categories. In addition, only one volunteer teacher held a professional teaching certificate, one an emergency certificate, and thirty-eight no certificate, although several were pursuing graduate study in education to become certified.

Among the full-time teaching staff who completed surveys were twenty men (33 percent) and forty-one women (67 percent). Sixty-nine percent of these teachers identified themselves as Caucasian and 26 percent as African American or black. With respect to certification status, 48 percent ($N = 29$) held a professional teaching certificate, 7 percent ($N = 4$) a provisional certificate, and one teacher an emergency certificate. Forty-four percent ($N = 27$) were not certified, although the vast majority were pursuing certification through master's degree programs. With respect to urban school teaching, full-time fully certified teachers reported 11.6 years experience, noncertified teachers 9.3 years, the four with provisional certification 3.8 years, and the one with emergency certification 8 years. Full-time teachers received salaries and benefits at, or slightly above, the level of parochial school teachers in their city.

COMPARISON SCHOOLS

The two comparison schools, which housed middle school programs within a larger Pre-K–8 coeducational school structure, were located in Baltimore, Maryland, and enrolled 84 boys and 103 girls in grades six through eight. Of the 116 students in one of the schools, all but one identified themselves as African American or black. The other comparison school had a more diverse student body with 59 percent of students self-identifying as African American or black, 28 percent as white, 6 percent as Hispanic, and 7 percent as biracial or other among the 71 participants in the study. The student–teacher ratio for the comparison schools was 20.7 to 1, the median class size for instruction was 22, and students attended school a mean of 7 hours per day. The mean age of the students was 12.6 years (SD = 1.0) and 90 percent qualified for federal free or reduced meals.

All eleven teachers (eight women and three men) who taught middle school students in the comparison schools completed teacher surveys. The median number of years of teaching among them was seventeen with a median of four in their current school. Eight of nine who responded indicated that they were certified and all eleven worked full time at the school. Four of the teachers identified themselves as African American or black, six as white, and 1 as biracial.

APPENDIX B

Procedures and Instruments

SCHOOL VISITS

I visited each of the eleven schools included in the study between October 2003 and April 2004. I spent some additional time in the Baltimore schools during the 2004–2005 and 2005–2006 academic years and made one half-day visit to the Boston school for boys in 2006 and the Milwaukee school in 2005. During the course of my visits, I conducted observations of classes and other school activities and interviewed administrators, teachers, and students at every school. I also interviewed graduates of the schools and parents where possible.

CLASSROOM AND SCHOOL OBSERVATIONS

I spent at least one full day, and usually part of a second day, at each school included in the study during which I visited four to six classes, attended the morning assembly, had lunch with students or faculty, and attended one or more afternoon or evening activities. I took notes in each class and performed a brief analysis of the learning climate of many of the classes.

INTERVIEWS

At each school, I conducted individual interviews with the school head or principal and, in most cases, the president or executive director, the development director, and the director of graduate support. I also conducted individual interviews with four or more teachers at each school, making sure to talk with teachers who were part of the full-time professional staff as well as those designated as volunteers, or interns. In addition, I interviewed two or more groups of students at each school, and, in most cases, one or more parents and graduates. Most of the interviews were voice recorded. Where I was not able to voice record the interviews, I took notes that I later typed up and filled in with information I recalled from the visit (usually within twenty-four hours). Table B.1 summarizes the number of students, teachers, administrators, parents, and alumni who participated in the study from the eleven Nativity schools.

QUESTIONNAIRES

Students and teachers completed questionnaires either prior to or following my visit to the school and a Teacher Evaluation of Student Behavior form was completed by one teacher who knew each student best.

STUDENT SURVEY

The 10-page student survey was administered by school personnel in classroom settings in the fall of 2003 or the spring of 2004. In addition to ten demographic items, the survey contained items and scales that assessed sev-

TABLE B.1
Types of Data Collected and Numbers of Participants
from Each Nativity School in 2003–2004

School	Std. Test Scores	Student Surveys	Teacher Surveys	Student Interview	Teacher Interview	Admin Interview	Parent Interview	Alumni Interview
NYCB	41	56	8	6	5	3	1	3 (also teachers)
BOSB	0	54	12	2	4	4	0	0
BALB	51	68	10	8	4	4	3	1
MILB	32	51	8	4	7	4	10	4
NYCG	31	51	6	16	5	3	3	2
BOSG	0	0	0	14	3	4	1	0
BALC	58	64	7	24	4	5	0	3
NORB	0	48	6	0	8	3	2	2
BOSC	40	77	20	7	5	5	0	1
WASG	26	47	10	14	4	4	3	2
STPC	36*	0	0	3	4	4	0	0
Totals	315	516	87	98	53	43	23	18

Note: *Data collected in Summer 2002, for the class of 2002, is examined. No test score data were provided by the school in 2003–2004.

eral aspects of students' perceptions, attitudes, and behaviors. Eighteen items, taken from an evaluation instrument developed by the Center for Research on the Education of Students Placed At Risk (CRESPAR) at Johns Hopkins University for the evaluation of the Talent Development Middle Schools, assessed students' perceptions of the quality of the social climate at their school. Other scales adapted from the CRESPAR instrument include assessments of students' perceived level of engagement in school (five items), their perceived difficulty of adjusting to school this year (four items), their perceptions of their parents' levels of engagement in their schooling (eight items, broken into two subscales of involvement and support), and their perceptions of the learning climate in their math class and in their English/language arts class (six items each combined into a single scale). These scales use a four-point forced-choice response format with responses indicating the extent to which the student disagrees or agrees with a given statement.

Finally, a twenty-three-item scale was included to assess students' perceptions of their self-worth (seven items, adapted from Harter, 1985), intrinsic motivation (twelve items, adapted from Harter, 1981), and commitment to helping other people (four items) using a four-point, *Strongly Disagree—Strongly Agree* response format. Factor analyses and alpha reliability analyses led to the removal of a few items from some of the scales to maximize their internal reliability levels and construct validity. The scales used in the analyses included in the present study with their alpha reliability coefficients are listed in Table B.2.

Teacher Assessment of Students

A Teacher Evaluation of Student Behavior form was completed for each student by the student's homeroom teacher or primary advisor. The form consists of thirty items that address the level of students' cooperativeness, completion of learning tasks, leadership, and acting-out behaviors. Teachers indicated whether the quality or behavior is *true* of the student over the previous six weeks *not at all* (coded 0), *somewhat* or *sometimes* (coded 1), or *very much* or *very often* (coded 2). Ten items were extracted from this measure for use in the present study that assessed the teacher's perception of the level of the student's academic engagement (e.g., the student works well independently, is interested in class material, complete assignments on time).

Teacher Survey

Surveys administered to teachers were mailed to each school included in the study. Instructions on the surveys directed teachers to complete them and return them in a postage-paid envelope directly to Loyola College to ensure the confidentiality of their responses. On this survey, respondents indicated the nature of their teaching assignment, including nonteaching duties, any

TABLE B.2

Variables Assessed from Scales Derived from Student and Teacher Surveys

Variable (Scale)	Number of items	Alpha Reliability
Student Self-Perceptions		
Self-Esteem	6	.76
Intrinsic Motivation for School	7	.80
School Adjustment Difficulty	5	.90
Student Climate Perceptions		
Principal Is Caring and Supportive	3	.71
Peer Social Climate	4	.68
School Enjoyable/Rules Fair	5	.78
Math and Language Arts		
Class Learning Climate	12	.79
Parent Involvement	4	.78
Parent Support	4	.68
Teacher Evaluation of Students		
Student Academic Engagement	10	.89
Teacher Climate and Self-Perceptions		
Engages Students in Learning	7	.72
Feels Supported by Administration	7	.74

certifications they held, and the number of years of teaching experience they have had at their present school, any urban school, and all schools. Teachers also responded to items that assessed their perceptions of the quality of their work environment and school climate, including assessments of the support they receive from administration, the commitment of their colleagues, how well teachers and administrators function as a team, and how well the school lives its mission (nineteen items in all). In addition, teachers reported the extent to which they received the instructional materials they needed (two items) and adequate professional development opportunities and mentoring (four items), as well as how they perceive the extent to which they motivate and care for their students (thirteen items). Teachers also responded to seven items, specific to the subject matter they teach, regarding some of their instructional techniques, such as the use of group projects or discussions, time spent on student discipline, and the extent to which they coordinate course content with that of other classes. Much of the questionnaire was adapted from one used and shared by the researchers at CRESPAR. On the questionnaire, teachers also were given the opportunity to respond to open-ended items regarding their perceptions of the strengths and shortcomings of the school and why they chose to teach at the school. Two scales from the teacher survey developed from factor analyses and used in this study are shown in Table B.2.

CLASS OBSERVATIONS

Provided with a schedule of classes at each school, I observed at least part of forty-six classes of forty-two different teachers, 67 percent of whom were experienced full-time teachers. Of these classes, twenty-five were observed for thirty minutes or more, representing fourteen experienced and eleven volunteer teachers. A modified version of the Classroom Environment Scale (CES; Moos & Trickett, 1987) was used to guide the recording of teacher and student behaviors in these classes. The modified form included items that addressed behaviors that could be observed during a thirty- to fifty-minute class period. The CES scales used included: (a) *Involvement,* or the level of engagement of students in the lesson (nine items); (b) *Teacher support,* or the extent to which teachers demonstrated respect for and desire to help students (nine items); (c) *Task orientation,* or the extent to which students were on task (eight items); (d) *Teacher control,* or how well the teacher managed student classroom behavior (eight items), and (e) *Order and organization,* or the extent to which the teacher began class on time, students were in their seats ready to begin work, and the teacher made effective transitions between instructional activities (nine items). A three-point response scale (scored 2, 1, or 0) was used for the observer to record whether a particular behavior was *Really True, Somewhat True,* or *Not True* for the teacher or students in the class. A teacher was then rated as *High* on a scale if a score of at least 14 on a nine-item scale or 13 on an eight-item scale (approximately 80 percent of the maximum score) was recorded, *Moderate* if a score between 11 and 13 on a nine-item scale or between 10 and 12 on an eight-item scale (between 60 percent and 80 percent of the maximum score) was recorded, and *Low* if a score lower than 10 on a nine-item scale and 9 on an eight-item scale was recorded. Reliability for this modified CES was established in an earlier study (Fenzel, Peyrot, & Premoshis, 1997) and verified by having two raters independently evaluate teaching in three classes from the present study.

SCHOOL DATA FORM

I devised a three-page form that was mailed to school directors or presidents on which respondents provided information on structural aspects of the schools, including enrollments in each grade, racial/ethnic makeup of the student population, the budget for salaries and operating costs, the numbers of teachers and administrators, paid and unpaid, the number of applicants for the most recently admitted class, the length of the school day, average class size for instruction, and the cocurricular activities offered students. Of the eleven schools included in this study, school data forms were completed and returned by seven schools. I obtained the information needed from schools that did not complete a form during interviews with school administrators.

ACADEMIC AND ATTENDANCE RECORDS

One of the school administrators at each school was asked to complete a Student Record Form for each student currently enrolled in grades six through eight and for the class of 2003 (the most recent graduating class). On this form, respondents recorded students' total mathematics and reading scores from standardized tests taken in grades five (when available), six, and seven, as well as final report card grades in math, language arts, and science and number of days absent from school for all years the student attended the school. Only ID numbers were recorded on these forms. These numbers corresponded to names of students kept on a separate and secure list to ensure student confidentiality. These forms were completed by personnel at seven of the eleven Nativity schools included in this study. Data provided by one additional school one year prior to the present study was used in some of the analyses.

COMPARISON SCHOOLS

I selected two parochial schools in Baltimore to serve as comparison schools for the study. Both schools were located in city neighborhoods where levels of unemployment, economic poverty, and drug abuse were relatively high. This type of neighborhood environment was more characteristic of one of the comparison schools. Both schools are coeducational Pre–8 schools for which tuition covers roughly one-third of the school's operational budget. Both Title I schools, their budgets constrained the breadth of their curricular and cocurricular offerings for students. These schools served as effective comparison schools in that they each have a history of high attendance, good-quality teaching, and excellent leadership. The percentage of students in the comparison schools who qualified for the federal free and reduced price meal program (90 percent) was slightly lower than that of the group of Nativity schools.

At these schools, students and teachers completed the written surveys described above and principals completed the School Data Form and academic and attendance data for each child in grades six through eight. No interviews or formal class observations were conducted, although I spent a small amount of time in each of the schools, speaking informally with the principals and teachers.

APPENDIX C

Attendance Rates and Standardized Test Results for Individual Schools

(Percent of Students Who Achieve at the Indicated Level)

School Code	Attendance Rate in 7th Grade	Reading: Gain ≥ 1 GE/year[1]	Math: Gain ≥ 1 GE/year[1]	7th Reading at or above grade level[2]	7th Math at or above grade level[2]
NYCG	97.6%	0.89	0.74	0.79	0.86
BOSC	98.9%	0.79	0.66	0.53	0.53
NYCB	98.4%	0.84	0.78	0.57	0.43
BALC	97.3%	0.75	0.65	0.36	0.35
BALB	97.5%	0.72	0.40	0.85	0.69
MILB	99.3%	0.66	0.80	0.94	0.94
WASG	94.3%	0.40	0.40	0.38	0.44
STPC[+]	96.2%	0.29	0.34	0.33	0.36
COM1*	97.2%	0.71	0.33	0.38	0.21
COM2*	97.0%	0.44	0.42	0.23	0.24

Notes: [+]2001–2002 data (all other data collected in 2003–2004 for the 2002–2003 school year).

[1]Proportion of students showing grade equivalent (GE) gains in standardized test scores equal to or greater than the number of years they attended the school. [2]Proportion of students scoring at or above grade level (GL) at the time of test administration.

*Denotes comparison parochial school.

APPENDIX D

Comparison of Means of Student Self-Perceptions and Perceptions of Environment for Eight Nativity and Two Traditional Parochial Schools

Student Perceptions (Total N = 654)	Nativity Schools (N = 467)	Comparison Schools (N = 187)	t	Cohen's d
Self-Esteem	3.37 (.49)[1]	3.50 (.58)	−2.88*	.23
Intrinsic Motivation	2.98 (.56)	3.07 (.58)	−1.86	.15
School Adjustment Difficulty	2.92 (1.19)	3.01 (1.16)	−0.85	.07
Principal Caring and Supportive	3.40 (.53)	3.58 (.57)	−3.92**	.31
Peer Social Climate	3.20 (.54)	2.97 (.52)	5.13**	.40
School is Enjoyable and Rules Fair	3.12 (.60)	2.84 (.61)	5.34**	.42
Math and LA Class Climate	3.08 (.41)	2.90 (.43)	5.14**	.40

Note: [1]Standard Deviation.

Two-tailed values: *$p \leq .01$, **$p \leq .001$.

References

Abell Foundation. (2001, October). Teacher certification: An idea whose time has gone. *The Abell Report, 14*(5), 1–4.

Alliance for Excellent Education. (2003a, May). *The building blocks of success for America's middle and high school students.* Washington, DC: Author. Policy Brief retrieved from http://www.all4ed.org/publications/BuildingBlocksofSuccess.doc.

Alliance for Excellent Education. (2003b, November). *Left behind: Six million at-risk secondary students.* Washington, DC: Author. Issue Brief retrieved from http://www.all4ed.org/publications/SixMillionKids.pdf.

Balfanz, R., & Byrnes, V. (2006). Closing the mathematics achievement gap in high-poverty middle schools: Enablers and constraints. *Journal of Education for Students Placed at Risk, 11*, 143–159.

Balfanz, R., & Mac Iver, D. (2000). Transforming high-poverty urban middle schools into strong learning institutions: Lessons for the first five years of the Talent Development Middle School. *Journal of Education for Students Placed at Risk, 5*, 137–158.

Barton, P. E. (2003, October). *Parsing the achievement gap: Baselines for tracking progress.* Princeton, NJ: Educational Testing Service.

Borman, G. D., Benson, J., & Overman, L. T. (2005). Families, schools, and summer learning. *The Elementary School Journal, 106*, 131–150.

Bradford, D. J. (1999). Exemplary middle school teachers' use of the five standards of effective teaching. *Teaching and Change, 7*, 53–78.

Brody, G. H., Ge, X., Dim, S. Y., Murry V. M., Simons, R. L., Gibbons, F. X., et al. (2003). Neighborhood disadvantage moderates associations of parenting and older sibling problem attitudes and behavior with conduct disorders in African American children. *Journal of Counseling and Clinical Psychology, 71*, 211–222.

Carnegie Council on Adolescent Development. (1989). *Turning points: Preparing American youth for the 21st century.* New York: Carnegie Corporation of New York.

Cochran-Smith, M. (2003). Teaching quality matters. *Journal of Teacher Education*, *54*, 95–98.

Cooper, H., Nye, B., Charlton, K, Lindsay, J., & Greathouse, S. (1996). The effects of summer vacation on achievement test scores: A narrative and meta-analytic review. *Review of Educational Research*, *66*, 227–268.

Cose, E. (2004, May 17). Brown v. board: A dream deferred. *Newsweek*, *143*(20), 52–59.

Council of Great City Schools. (2003, May 15). *Urban school coalition calls for federal action to address school resource disparities*. Press release retrieved from http://www.cgcs.org/pressrelease/2003/5-15-03.html.

Darling-Hammond, L. (2000). Teacher quality and student achievement: A review of state policy evidence. *Education Policy Analysis Archives*, *8*(1). Retrieved February 14, 2005, from http://epaa.asu.edu/epaa/v8n1/.

Darling-Hammond, L. (2002, September 6). Research and rhetoric on teacher certification: A response to "Teacher Certification Reconsidered," *Education Policy Analysis Archives*, *10*(36). Retrieved July 22, 2004 from http://epaa.asu.edu/epaa/v10n36.html.

Decker, P. T., Mayer, D. P., & Glazerman, S. (2004). *The effects of Teach for America on students: Findings from a national evaluation*. Princeton, NJ: Mathematica Policy Research. Retrieved December 12, 2006, from http://www.teachforamerica.org/documents/mathematica_results_6.9.04.pdf.

Delpit, L. (2006a). Lessons from teachers. *Journal of Teacher Education*, *57*, 220–231.

Delpit, L. (2006b). *Other people's children: Cultural conflict in the classroom*. New York: New Press.

Eccles J. S., Wigfield, A., Midgley, C., Reuman, D., Mac Iver, D., & Feldlaufer, H. (1993). Negative effects of traditional middle schools on students' motivation. *The Elementary School Journal*, *93*, 553–574.

Editorial Projects in Education. (2007). *State information*. Retrieved December 8, 2006, from http://www2.edweek.org/rc/states/.

Epiphany (n.d.). *Our programs*. Retrieved December 8, 2006, from http://www.epiphanyschool.com/index.php.

Evans, G. W. (2004). The environment of childhood poverty. *American Psychologist*, *59*, 77–92.

Fenzel, L. M. (2003, June). *Report on an evaluation of selected Nativity schools*. Baltimore: Loyola College in Maryland. Unpublished document.

Fenzel, L. M., Domingues, J., & Raughley, B. (2006, April). *Educating at-risk urban African American children: A comparison of the effectiveness of two types of middle schools*. Paper presented at the annual meeting of the American Educational Research Association, San Francisco.

Fenzel, L. M., & Flippen, G. M. (2006, April). *Student engagement and the use of volunteer teachers in alternative urban middle schools*. Paper presented at the annual meeting of the American Educational Research Association, San Francisco.

Fenzel, L. M., Magaletta, P. R., & Peyrot, M. F. (1997). The relationship of school strain to school functioning and self-worth among urban African American early adolescents. *Psychology in the Schools, 34*, 1–10.

Fenzel, L. M., & Monteith, R. H. (2008). Successful alternative middle schools for urban minority children: A study of Nativity schools. *Journal of Education for Students Placed at Risk, 13*, 381–401.

Fenzel, L. M., & O'Brennan, L. M. (2007, April). *Educating at-risk urban African American children: The effects of school climate on motivation and academic achievement.* Paper presented at the annual meeting of the American Educational Research Association, Chicago.

Fenzel, L. M., Peyrot, M., & Premoshis, K. (1997, March). *Alternative model for urban middle level schooling: An evaluation study.* Paper presented at the annual meeting of the American Educational Research Association, Chicago, IL. ERIC Document No. ED 409387.

George, P. S., & Alexander, W. M. (2003). *The exemplary middle school* (3rd ed.). Belmont, CA: Wadsworth.

Greene, J. P., & Forster, G. (2003). *Public high school graduation and college readiness rates in the United States.* New York: Manhattan Institute. Retrieved February 14, 2006, from http://www.manhattan-institute.org/html/ewp_03.htm#01.

Hale, J. E. (2001). *Learning while black: Creating educational excellence for African American children.* Baltimore, MD: Johns Hopkins University Press.

Hans-Kolvenbach, P., S. J. (2001, Summer). As I see it: Father General's words on justice in higher education. *Company, 18*(4), 30–31.

Harter, S. (1981). A new self-report scale of intrinsic versus extrinsic orientation in the classroom: Motivational and informational components. *Developmental Psychology, 17*, 300–312.

Harter, S. (1985). *Manual for the Self-Perception Profile for Children* (Unpublished manuscript). Boulder, CO: University of Denver.

Hendrie, C. (2004, January 21). In U.S. schools, race still counts. *Education Week.* Retrieved January 15, 2005, from http://www.edweek.org/ew/ewstory.cfm?slug= 19Brown.h23.

Ingersoll, R. M. (2001). Teacher turnover and teacher shortages: An organizational analysis. *American Educational Research Journal, 38*, 499–534.

Jackson, A. W., & Davis, G. A. (2000). *Turning points 2000: Educating adolescents in the 21st century.* New York: Teachers College Press.

Jencks, C., & Phillips, M. (1998). *The Black-White test score gap.* Washington, DC: Brookings Institution Press.

Jesuit Secondary Education Association. (n.d.). *The characteristics of a Jesuit education.* Retrieved December 14, 2006, from http://sjweb.info/education/documents/ characteristics_en.doc.

Joftus, S. (2002, September). *Every child a graduate: A framework for an excellent education for all middle and high school students.* Washington, DC: Alliance for Excellent Education.

Kaplan, A. S., & Owings, W. A. (2001). Teacher quality and student achievement: Recommendations for principals. *National Association of Secondary School Principals. NASSP Bulletin, 85,* 64–73.

Keller, B. (2007, April). Cultures of commitment. *Education Week, 26*(33), 24–27.

KIPP Foundation. (2007). *About KIPP.* Retrieved January 10, 2007, from http://www.kipp.org.

Kopetz, P. B., Lease, A. J., & Warren-Kring, B. Z. (2006). *Comprehensive urban education.* Boston: Pearson.

Kozol, J. (2005). *The shame of the nation: The restoration of apartheid schooling in America.* New York: Crown.

Kunjufu, J. (1989). *Critical issues in educating African American youth.* Chicago: African American Images.

Laczko-Kerr, I., & Berliner, D. C. (2002, September 6). The effectiveness of "Teach for America" and other under-certified teachers on student academic achievement: A case of harmful public policy. *Education Policy Analysis Archives, 10*(37). Retrieved January 15, 2005, from http://epaa.asu.edu/epaa/v10n37/.

Lewis, A. C. (2000). A tale of two reform strategies. In J. Norton & A. C. Lewis, *Middle grades reform: A Kappan special report, 81,* K1–K20. Retrieved March 15, 2004, from http://www.pdkintl.org/kappan/klew0006.htm.

Lipsitz, J. (1984). *Successful schools for young adolescents.* New Brunswick, NJ: Transaction Books.

Mac Iver, D. J., Ruby, A., Balfanz, R., & Byrnes, V. (2003). Removed from the list: A comparative longitudinal case study of a reconstitution-eligible school. *Journal of Curriculum and Supervision, 18,* 259–289.

Maryland State Department of Education (2003, February). *Quality teacher work group final report.* Retrieved March 15, 2004, from http://www.marylandpublicschools.org/NR/rdonlyres/B1785244–ACED-4631–B6A1–03C51E7AAC2A/1501/Quality_Teacher_Report.pdf.

Massachusetts Department of Education. (2006). *FY05 per pupil expenditures: Day programs.* Retrieved December 12, 2006, from http://finance1.doe.mass.edu/statistics/pp05.html.

Moos, R. H., & Trickett, E. J. (1987). *Classroom Environment Scale manual* (2nd ed.). Palo Alto, CA: Consulting Psychologists Press.

Mother Seton Academy (2005). *Mother Seton Academy: A holistic approach to Catholic middle school education: Program.* Retrieved December 21, 2005, from http://www.mothersetonacademy.org.

Murrell, P. C., Jr. (2008). Toward social justice in urban education: A model of collaborative cultural inquiry in urban schools. In F. P. Peterman (Ed.), *Partnering to prepare urban teachers: A call to activism* (pp. 41–57). New York: Peter Lang.

National Center for Educational Statistics. (1996). *Urban schools: The challenge of location and poverty.* Jessup, MD: U.S. Department of Education. Ed Pubs # NCES 96–184.

National Center for Educational Statistics. (2003). *The condition of education 2003*, NCES 2003–067, Washington, DC: U.S. Government Printing Office.

National Center for Educational Statistics. (2004a). *The nation's report card: Mathematics highlights 2003. Fourth- and eighth-graders' average mathematics scores increase.* Jessup, MD: U.S. Department of Education. Ed Pubs # NCES 2004–451.

National Center for Educational Statistics. (2004b). *The nation's report card: Reading highlights 2003. Average fourth- and eighth-grade reading scores show little change.* Jessup, MD: U.S. Department of Education. Ed Pubs # NCES 2004–452.

National Center for Educational Statistics. (2004c). *Digest of educational statistics, 2004: Chapter 2. Elementary and secondary education.* Retrieved December 21, 2006, from http://nces.ed.gov/programs/digest/do4/tables/dt04_060.asp.

National Middle School Association. (2003). *This we believe: Successful schools for young adolescents.* Westerville, OH: Author.

Nativity Mission Center. (2003–2004). *Nativity Student/Parent Handbook.*

Nativity Network. (n.d.). *About the Nativity Educational Centers Network.* Retrieved March 10, 2006, from http://www.nativitynetwork.org/about/index.html.

NativityMiguel Network of Schools. (2007, July 16). *Executive summary report: School year 2006–07.* Washington, DC: Author.

NativityMiguel Network of Schools. (n.d.). *Overview.* Retrieved January 10, 2007, from http://www.nativitymiguelschools.org/about_schools/overview.shtml.

Ness, M. (2004). *Lessons to learn: Voices from the front lines of Teach for America.* New York: RoutledgeFalmer.

Newman, F. M., & Oliver, D. W. (1967). Education and community. *Harvard Educational Review, 37*(1), 61–106.

Noguera, P. A. (2003). *City schools and the American dream: Reclaiming the promise of public education.* New York: Teachers College Press.

Noguera, P. (2005). The racial achievement gap: How can we assure an equity of outcomes? In L. Johnson, M. E. Finn, & R. Lewis (Eds.), *Urban education with an attitude* (pp. 1–7). Albany: State University of New York Press.

Norton, J. (2000). Important developments in middle-grades reform. In J. Norton & A. C. Lewis, *Middle grades reform: A Kappan special report, 81*, K1–K20. Retrieved March 2, 2004, from http://www.pdkintl.org/kappan/klew0006.htm.

Podsiadlo, Rev. J. J., S.J., & Philliber, W. W. (2003). The Nativity Mission Center: A successful approach to the education of Latino boys. *Journal of Education for Students Placed at Risk, 8*, 419–428.

President's Advisory Commission on Educational Excellence for Hispanic Americans. (2003, March). *From risk to opportunity: Fulfilling the educational needs of Hispanic Americans in the 21st century.* White House Initiative on Educational Excellence for Hispanic Americans. Retrieved August 21, 2005, from http://www/yesican.gov/paceea/final.html.

Prince, C. D. (2002). Missing: Top staff in bottom schools. *School Administrator, 59*(7), 6–9, 11–14.

Putnam, R. D. (2001). *Bowling alone: The collapse and revival of American community*. New York: Simon and Schuster.

Raymond, M., Fletcher, S. H., & Luque, J. (2001, August). *Teach for America: An evaluation of teacher differences and student outcomes in Houston, Texas*. Stanford, CA: Center for Research on Educational Outcomes, the Hoover Institution, Stanford University.

Renaissance Learning (2006). *Accelerated Reader enterprise*. Retrieved December 10, 2006, from http://www.renlearn.com/ar/default.htm.

Rist, R. C. (2000). Student social class and teacher expectations: The self-fulfilling prophecy in ghetto education. *Harvard Educational Review, 70*, 257–301.

Robelen, E. W. (2007, June 13). KIPP student attrition patterns eyed. *Education Week, 26*(41), 1, 16–17.

Ruby, A. (2006). Improving science achievement at high-poverty urban middle schools. *Science Education, 90*, 1005–1027.

Simmons, R. G., & Blyth, D. A. (1987). *Moving into adolescence: The impact of pubertal change and school context*. New York: Aldine.

Smith, S. L., & Smith, B. J. (2006). Perceptions of violence: The views of teachers who left urban schools. *The High School Journal, 9*(3), 34–42.

Society of Jesus (1994–1995). *The decrees of General Congregation Thirty-Four, the fifteenth of the restored society and the accompanying papal and Jesuit documents*. Rome, Italy: Curia of the Superior General. Retrieved from http://www.jesuit.org.

Society of the Holy Child Jesus (2002). *Welcome: Home page of the Society of the Holy Child Jesus*. Retrieved from http://www.shcj.org/shcj.nsf/pages/Home.

Storz, M. G., & Nestor, K. R. (2008). It's all about relationships: Urban middle school students speak out on effective schooling practices. In F. P. Peterman (Ed.), *Partnering to prepare urban teachers: A call to activism* (pp. 77–101). New York: Peter Lang.

Thernstrom, A., & Thernstrom, S. (2003). *No excuses: Closing the racial gap in learning*. New York: Simon & Schuster.

Town Hall Education, Arts, & Recreation Campus. (2006). *THEARC: About us*. Retrieved from http://thearcdc.org/about/index.asp.

Trimble, S. (2004). *What works to improve student achievement*. NMSA Research Summary #20. Retrieved from http://www.nmsa.org/research/summary/studentachievement.htm.

U. S. Census Bureau. (2006, March). *Public education finances, 2004*. Retrieved from http://www.census.gov/govs/www/school.html.

Wilson, B. L., & Corbett, H. D. (2001). *Listening to urban kids: School reform and the teachers they want*. Albany: State University of New York Press.

Author Index

Subject Index